Apostolic Intervention

(A Biblical and Contemporary Overview of the Apostolic Impact upon European, Ancient, and American Cities)

Apostle Dr. Elizabeth A. Hairston

(Foreword by Dr. Bill Hamon)

xulon PRESS

For ordering information, permission, or questions contact:

Apostle Elizabeth A. Hairston, PhD
P. O. Box 541564
Opa-Locka, Florida 33054

(305) 654-9059
E-mail: Aposprop@bellsouth.net

Dedication

My great grandson

Marquez Micah Phillip Brown

Acknowledgments

My best friend and Senior Pastor of Rose of Sharon Ministries, Pastor Sherron Parrish

Pastor Christine Long, who opened her lovely home for me to complete this work

Prophetess Kim Neuhaus

Apostle Ronald Harden

My daughters, Minister Constance Marie Brown McIntyre and Charlotte Elizabeth Evans

My granddaughter, Makeda Elizabeth Nichols

My grandson, Robert Evans, Jr.

Derryl-Ann Adams

The Rose of Sharon Ministries Family

Table of Contents

Dedication...v

Acknowledgments...vii

Foreword...xi

Introduction xiii

Chapter I: The City – An Understanding 15

Chapter II: Cain – The Ancient Builder..21

Chapter III: Noah – Intervener Of A Nameless City 25

Chapter IV: Nimrod – Building On His Own Foundation 31

Chapter V: Abraham – Apostolic Pursuit For A City With Foundations...........................37

Chapter VI: Moses – Intervener In A Wilderness...43

Chapter VII: Nehemiah – Governmental Intervention 51

Chapter VIII: Apostles – Interrupting Religious And Economic Systems..........................59

Chapter IX: The JEDAH Company – Women Building With Network Focus 65

Chapter X: Apostolic Emancipators 77

Chapter XI: Marketplace Trailblazers – Cutting The Edge Of Slavery 85

Chapter XII: 20th – 21st Century Apostles Impacting The Cities 93

    Responses To Survey 93

    Endnotes 115

    Bibliography 117

    Additional Books By The Author..119

Foreword

by Dr. Bill Hamon

T here are those whom God calls to pioneer specific truths and restoration of ministries back into the Church. Elizabeth Hairston is one of those whom God has called and commissioned as an Apostle of Jesus Christ.

I believe and have taught that Apostles and Prophets are active ministers in the present-day Church. I have prophesied five-fold ministry calling to thousands of people during my 50 years of ministry. Romans 12:6 declares that we prophesy according to the proportion of our faith. There was a time when I only had faith to prophesy to women a five-fold calling of Evangelist, Teacher, Pastor, or Prophet. Because of traditional church doctrine, I did not have the faith to prophesy an Apostolic calling to women.

Faith comes from an accurate revelation and application of the Word of God. The Holy Spirit finally made real to me that each of the five-fold ascension gifts of Christ is a co-equal ministry of the One Christ! No scripture exalts one gift or calling above the other. Each of the five are one-fifth of the total Christ; Christ is not in competition with Himself, nor is He in conflict concerning which part of His ministry is greatest or least. Therefore, if a woman can be called to express the life and ministry of Christ as an Evangelist or a Teacher, then a woman must be able to be called to express Christ as an Apostle.

Apostle Elizabeth Hairston is fully qualified to write about Apostolic Intervention. She is an Apostle with a special anointing to teach and demonstrate the ministry of Jesus Christ. May the scriptural truth, illustration, and life examples in this book bless all who read it.

God bless you, Apostle Hairston, for giving these beneficial truths to help us participate in Apostle Intervention according to the heart and mind of our Lord, Christ Jesus.

Dr. Bill Hamon, Founder and Chairman
Christian International Ministries Network
Santa Rosa Beach, Florida
www.christianinternational.org
Author of many major books
Most recent release The Day of the Saints

Introduction

Apostles entering and residing in cities, emerge as those who will change the spiritual, financial and political climate in that region. Apostles are men or women whom God chose to send to a specific group of people or many nations to, a geographical area to establish order, develop ideas and strategies to assess and sometimes restructure mindsets regarding biblical doctrine. They are considered as individuals who are the first to pioneer movements or forms of worship for a specific period of time.

Presently, Apostles and Prophets are not only establishing order, but they are preparing the Body of Christ to operate in its fullest potential so that it can be mobilized for the 21st century as a mighty army in the earth, so that the gifts Jesus gave to the church will begin to function as a unit. As Apostles and Prophets bring together the five-fold ministry, we can expect great results.

The evangelist will be able to move into foreign or virgin territory as a team because the Apostles will have pioneered the way for them.

Pastors will gather the overflowing harvest as the Evangelist preaches on the street, sidewalks, bowling alleys, trains, buses, and in the prisons.

As the souls enter into the church the Pastor/Teacher or Pastor and Teachers will nurture the new believers in the word, quickly sending them forth to help edify other saints.

This mobilization will produce a global revival that will make it possible for mankind to stand in the face of global war, economic change, and governmental collapse.

This great emerging will be known as the Saints movement. Laborers will no longer be few, as they move by divine order to bring the Body of Christ together.

Apostolic Intervention will play a major role in this. It is necessary for each city to be prepared for the coming moves of God. Commencing in the 21st Century, these men and women will upset the present status of the church, forcing the church to take its proper place in the local community.

This book will seek to address the role of the Apostles in the cities, types of Apostles in the Old Testament and Apostolic intervention in the New Testament to present day.

CHAPTER I

THE CITY –
AN UNDERSTANDING

According to the World Book Encyclopedia, [1] a typical city covered less than one square mile (2.6 kilometers) and had walls around it for protection against invaders. [2]

In some cultures, prior to the Middle Ages, even before the birth of Christ to present day, cities were surrounded by a wall with a gate for entrance and exit. The gate often defined the specific parameter for the actual square footage of the city. It was also customary for a watchman to stand guard in a tower, as well as elders at the gate to notify when the enemy was approaching or what and by whom transactions are being made at the gate. Often, major decisions were made at the gate, whether purchasing or redeeming property or determining who was trying to seek refuge in their city.

The political and religious definition for city reflects that of a group of people with a common interest, living in a common area or a group with a similar focus who convene often to live out their common focus.

TYPES OF CITIES

THE CHURCH

The church is a type of city. Matthew 5:14 reads, *"Ye are the light of the world. A city that is set on an hill cannot be hid."* **Cosmopolites** of people who represent cultures gather on a common day of the week for its main service, to give glory to God in a house of worship.

One might consider this terminology as metaphorical, because it may not seem to line up with our understanding of a city.

The prophet Isaiah calls this group of people *"the city of righteousness"* (Isaiah 1:21, 26) and **"faithful."**

THE BODY

The human body can be described as a city due to the intricate manner in which human beings are designed. Many cities have gates to mark entrance and exits, just as the human body possess gates:

1) Cranial Area – Head
2) Eyes (2)
3) Ears (2)
4) Nose (1)
5) Mouth (1)
6) Palms of hands (2)
7) Sexual Organs (1)
8) Bottom of feet (2)

17

Not only does the body possess gates, but it consists of the following properties:

1) 263 Bones
2) 600 Muscles
3) 970 Miles [3] of Blood Vessels
4) Elements also found in the body, also found in cities:
   a) Iron
   b) Sugar
   c) Salt
   d) Carbon
   e) Iodine
   f) Phosphorous
   g) Lime
   h) Calcium
   i) Water
5) 10,000,000 Nerves and Branches
6) A telephone security system [4] that relates to the brain instantly any known sound, taste, sight, touch, or smell.
7) Cells and nerve platelets act as police officers [5] protecting red blood cells

TEMPORARY DWELLINGS

Temporary dwellings may also be considered as designated places for dwelling, such as trailer cities and tents. For example, the Black Foot Tribe of the Native American Nations, for years, lived in the Valleys of the Dakota's, during summer and spring then migrated to the mountains for the duration of the winter season.

They lived in tents, but their villages were considered as cities. There they resided, bought, sold, and exercised religious freedom until settlers began to invade their territories. At this point, their religious freedom became a political issue because it threatened the puritan order and sometimes the Catholic order, depending on whether the later settlers were originating from European (German, Irish descent) or Spanish-European.

PERMANENT DWELLING

A city is a place designated or established by one or more persons for the purpose of permanent dwelling, buying and selling, building, exercising political and/or religious freedom, refuge, and education.

This type of city can be the length or width of ten blocks, similar to how Jerusalem in Israel is designed. It is known as a city compacted together. On the other hand, it may measure as large as Hong Kong, China, or New York, New York.

METROPOLIS

A metropolis is a main city of a state, country, or region, sometimes referred to as capitals. For example, Washington D.C. is the metropolis for the United States. Lagos is the main city of the country of Nigeria in West Africa. Naroibi is the main city of Kenya, an East African country. Jackson is the metropolis of the state of Mississippi and Tallahassee is the metropolis of the State of Florida.

Major decisions for the nations and states are determined in the metropolis of that region.

COSMOPOLITE

According to Webster's Illustrated Dictionary, a Cosmopolite is a city with a cosmopolitan (common to all the world) population where many cultures meet. [6]

Miami, Florida, like many other cosmopolitan cities in the U.S., embrace people of practically every continent on the globe, including independent countries, which are located in the seas or oceans operating independently as Islands, such as Mauritius in the Indian Ocean and Madagascar located about 500 miles west of Mauritius.

Oftentimes, cities exist within cities. As masses of people begin to move from other countries to Miami, city planning begins to establish smaller townships or cities within Miami to accommodate the growth of the city. There are cities within five to ten minutes distance of one another, such as, Carol City, Opa-Locka, and Hialeah. Each of these three are an integral part of many cities, which constitute the cosmopolite, which Miami has become.

Cities can offer security at the same time that they offer community, whether the dwelling affords a temporary or permanent home base.

CHAPTER II

CAIN – THE
ANCIENT BUILDER

In the beginning God created the Heaven and the Earth (Genesis 1:1). During a process of time, He also created man whom He called Adam and woman, noting that their name shall be Adam. They were set in the earth as husband and wife, indicating the establishment of the family as an institution. They dwelt in the garden that God created known as Eden. Due to disobedience to God, they were cast out of their place of abode where Adam farmed the land for provision.

Their firstborn was named Cain. Later, another son was born called Abel. Cain became a farmer and Abel became a shepherd. During a process of time, they both worshipped God in offering the first fruit of their labor. Abel's offering was accepted by God, but Cain's was rejected. Cain became very distraught until he became jealous and killed his brother Abel, becoming the first to murder on the earth.

After Cain murdered his brother Abel, he was sent out of God's presence to become a fugitive and a vagabond in the earth. During this time of wandering, he settled in the land of Nod, east of Eden.

Although he was habitating outside of God's presence, and would be considered a fugitive and a vagabond (Genesis 4:14), it was in this unsettled place that Cain determined to establish, marry, have a family, and possess the land.

According to biblical history, Cain built a city in the land of Nod and named it after his firstborn son, Enoch. It would be well to hear that this Enoch precedes the Enoch who walked so closely with God until he was translated into God's presence.

Several generations of Cain's dwelt in the city of Enoch. They are as follows:

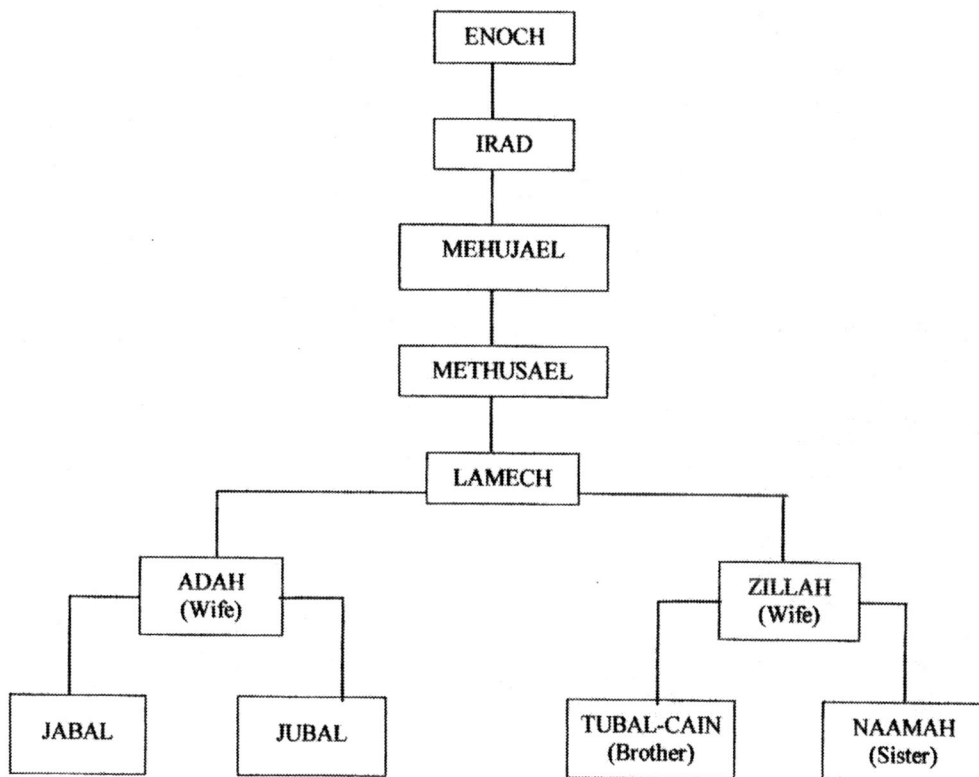

ENOCH

IRAD

MEHUJAEL

METHUSAEL

LAMECH

ADAH
(Wife)

ZILLAH
(Wife)

JABAL

JUBAL

TUBAL-CAIN
(Brother)

NAAMAH
(Sister)

OCCUPATION / INVENTIONS

Jabal (Nomad type Rancher): Father of such as dwelt in tents, and of such as have cattle.

Jubal (Creator of Instruments and Teacher of Music): Father of all, such as handle the harp and organs.

Tubal – Cain: Instructor of every Artificer in brass and iron.

From the loins of Cain came a nomadic rancher, a musical instrument inventor, a teacher of music, and a maker and teacher of brass and iron works (welder).

Interestingly enough, Cain's family is talented as musicians and instructors, there is no reference of those who worshipped God or made an altar to worship Him until their original father, Adam, brought forth a son whom they named Seth. According to the book of Genesis, Seth bore a son whom he called Enos and it was during that time that "men began to call upon the name of the Lord" (Genesis 4:26).

CHAPTER III

NOAH – INTERVENER
OF A NAMELESS CITY

According to biblical history, a man living in the earth during the century B.C., was the first to build an ark and an altar. He was given the name Noah, meaning rest, by his father Lamech.

Noah, meaning rest, was prophetically and Apostolically mandated to establish a place of safety for his family. This refuge was to be known as an ark. The purpose for the building of this ark, was to prepare not only a place of safety from the upcoming disaster of a flood, but to openly demonstrate to the people who would stop to hear him preach, that God is creator and must be respected and worshipped.

Noah is first to preach a message of repentance from a God who despises sin. The wickedness and corrupt living of mankind was so great until God Himself repented for making man.

In the midst of corruption, Noah found grace in God's sight. God considered Noah as a just man and perfect in his generation. Noah was given specific directions and instructions for building the ark and specific instructions as to how to prepare for worship after the flood.

Noah built the ark of gopher wood, which according to biblical archaeology was about the size of a football field. According to Lawrence Richardson, "the ark was a 450 x 75 x 45 foot vessel. The ark was built with three stories and one window." Obedience was absolutely necessary for Noah to walk in, as he was the only person in the proper position with God to rescue his family, a remnant from the flood.

Noah is also positioning himself at this critical time to set a precedence for worship. For God instructed Noah to bring two unclean beasts, fowl or creeping animal of each kind into the ark, but seven clean beasts. These clean beasts were to be brought so that Noah would have the proper and acceptable animals/fowls to offer as a sacrifice following the flood.

Two things we see taking place by Noah, which are Apostolic and prophetic:

1) An ark is built for safety and dwelling; and
2) An altar is built for worship.

Two Apostolic aspects of these two events are that Noah is the first to build the ark and the altar. Mankind prior to the flood did not utilize arks, for there had not been a need for them. However, worship had taken place prior to Noah as Cain and Abel made offerings unto God, but the record in Genesis does not indicate that Abel or Cain built an altar in relationship to worship.

Noah demonstrated that worship must be specific and intent because when God makes a promise, though you may face trials, there must be a place and a time to worship when the trial is over.

Noah, after spending one hundred years to build the ark, prepared the sacrifice for worship that would not be used for another one hundred and twenty days total.

This case scenario shows the believer that careful attention must be made when offerings are prepared, for worship unto God. This showed challenge for the twentieth or twenty-first century believer to determine how carefully they prepare offerings for the worship time at their churches. How far ahead offerings are prepared should be something to consider, though the time of some may not be for a preparation of four months, but time should be spent in preparation. Offerings are vehicles or instruments whereby God measures our hearts to see if our intent is for worship towards Him or ourselves.

Noah intervened or brought conflict in a city whose name is not mentioned in scripture, but from the city, the ark was launched forth into deep waters.

Landing on the top of Mount Ararat, which is present day Turkey. Noah needed a "helps ministry" to operate for him. At this point, Noah was positioning himself to be re-established in the earth. The process would require an investigation of the status of the land.

The ark rested on Mount Ararat, which is presently considered as Eastern Turkey, or Armenia, which according to Josephus means "The Place of Descent," the proper rendering of the city. He continues by saying:

> *"It is called in Ptolemy Naxuana, and by Moses Chorenesis, the Armenian historian, Idshauan; but at the place itself, Nachidsheuan, which signified the first place of descent, and is a lasting monument of the preservation of Noah in the ark, upon the top of that mountain at whose foot it was built, as the first city or town after the flood."* [7]

Not only did Noah build or established an ark and an altar, but he also established a city. However, before the city could be established, as mentioned earlier, the "helps ministry" came into focus to assist in preparation for rebuilding. Noah chose a raven to send out and assess the land. The raven, being considered as an unclean fowl, has no difficulty coming in contact with and eating dead or defiled flesh. Certainly as the waters receded, the raven would find a resting place readily.

Later, Noah sent a dove, typifying how after Jesus ascended, He also descended and gave gifts to men (Ephesians 4:8-11). Following His ascent to His Father, He sent the Holy Spirit to the earth. When Apostles send individuals out to do a work, they are expecting a deposit from those sent out. When the dove went out, he returned because he found no resting place; however, after seven more days, Noah sent the dove again, which returned in the evening with a deposit. In his mouth was a sign of hope, of life, an olive branch plucked from a tree. The olive branch speaks clearly of the following:

OLD TESTAMENT SYMBOLS	NEW TESTAMENT SYMBOLS
The waters are abated	The trial is over
The Olive tree remains. It is alive.	Jesus is Lord
The Spirit of God has blown across the land	The Holy Spirit is poured out
Noah establishes worship	The church is established
The earth's baptism is completed	Apostolic doctrine of repentance / and baptism is instituted

The dove is free now to rest in the land, even as the Holy Spirit (rushing wind) was poured out or sent to the earth on the day of Pentecost to rest upon the new believers who sat in the upper room. After receiving the Holy Spirit, they descended from the upper room. The Apostle confirmed the event with scripture exhortation and the church was born. Similarly, Noah and the eight people who were saved from the destruction of the flood experienced a form of baptism which prepared them for a worship experience.

Here a worship experience takes place that would, for centuries to come, impact all of humanity. Noah built an altar and he worshipped by carefully selecting an offering for God that would be acceptable. Seven clean animals were selected prior to the flood. This pre-selection suggests that Noah moved in faith, believing that he and all on the ark would remain safe throughout the flood. These offerings were placed on the altar that he built.

Worship includes submitting an offering of ourselves unto God or our substance. The seven clean animals symbolize a perfect sacrifice of his substance.

When Noah submitted the sacrifice to God and it was accepted, God exemplified His approval of Noah's obedience, by making Noah a promise not to send a flood to the earth again. He sealed his promise with a covenant. This is represented as a bow in the clouds. For the Lord said:

> *"I do set my bow in the cloud, and it shall be for a token of a covenant between me and the earth. And it shall come to pass when I bring a cloud over the earth, that the bow shall be seen in the cloud: and, I will remember my covenant, which is between me and you and every living creature of all flesh; and the waters shall no more, become a flood to destroy all flesh."*
> *Genesis 9:13-15*

Though Noah built the ark in a city whose name is not given, the covenant of the rainbow today is shown in many cities all over the world periodically as a reminder that God remembered His covenant with Noah, upon his descent from the ark, a new city for a new beginning, "The Place of Descent."

CHAPTER IV

NIMROD – BUILDING ON HIS OWN FOUNDATION

A good foundation is very crucial for any form of structure or building. Not only is a foundation crucial, but it is important for effectiveness.

Following the flood in Noah's day, his descendants began to replenish the earth. They spoke one language, and began to move upon the face of the earth in a land called Shinar.

The generations of Noah, which constituted these people, were Ham, Shem and Japheth. From the lineage of Ham proceedeth the Cushite nation from which came forth Nimrod, a mighty hunter in the earth. Nimrod even in his rebellion was a great builder. On the other hand, Nimrod was a rebel. God had served Adam and Eve with a mandate to replenish the earth. Obviously the order remained in force for the generation of Noah, since eight were saved during the flood. However, Nimrod and his generation chose to maintain in the land of Shinar and build a tower to reach Heaven, for fear that they would lose their identity.

These people feared being scattered, therefore began building a foundation on fear and rebellion. These two spirits are contrary to the Apostolic work. Though Nimrod had an Apostolic characteristic of being able to gather people, instruct them, share a plan, build a structure and raise up a nation, he was moving outside of God's direction, favor and anointing.

Nimrod, as a hunter had understood that God existed but we do not see evidence that he acknowledged or worshipped God. Genesis 10:9 states that Nimrod *"was a mighty hunter before the Lord,"* The Septuagint says he *"was a mighty hunter against the Lord."*

Whether for or against, Nimrod was knowledgeable of the Lord. Though knowledgeable of the Lord, Nimrod did not acknowledge Him as he purposed to build a tower with the intent of reaching God through his own selfish motives.

This project that Nimrod established provoked God the Father, God the Son and God the Holy Ghost, to come down and arrest the project. Here we see a powerful Apostolic intervention (Genesis11:1-8). Intervention means to "interfere in the affairs of one country by another by force or threat," or to "interfere with the acts of others."

The Lord, being the chief Apostle, although he had not physically come to the earth to serve in that capacity, initially, He came to assess the matter at hand, which is a major Apostolic characteristic. He then learned that the people's strength and ability to work together was strong, to the point that nothing would be impossible for them. As a result, He included the Father, who is the founder of building cities (Hebrews) and the Holy Spirit, the person of the Godhead who operates in creative power, when they went down to see the city and the tower, the strategy was to confuse their language and scatter the people abroad. Certainly the Apostolic strategy was effective and the people were scattered. To maintain this separation for a season, the earth was also divided at this time. Today these bodies of land, as opposed to one landmass, separated by water, are called continents.

The Apostolic/Prophetic team of God's kingdom defined the city then as Babel, because their language was confounded.

An analogy of the church can be drawn in this situation as we consider unity, building and visitation from God. Apostles have the ability to bring unity in the body; however, in this scenario, we have concluded that the behavior of Nimrod is not acceptable for an Apostle, although he established unity and began to build Babel and later build other cities, such as Erech, Accad and Calnah in the same land of Shinar. But in this scenario we can reflect on the need for unity in the church. The need is great. The church should have one mind and that is to glorify God, obey His will and promote His kingdom. An example of an acceptable building project is reflected in II Chronicles 5:13-14, when the glory of God descended upon the musicians and singers as they all began to minister as one. The power of God was so great until the priests could not stand to minister. The project's acceptance is confirmed by the outpouring of God's glory, which is equivalent to a visitation from God. Notice the contrast between building with God's approval to that of building outside of God's approval as demonstrated with Nimrod's Project. Note the order here:

SOLOMON'S BUILDING PROJECT

Build in Unity

Worshipped in Unity

Visitation from God – Glorious Intervention

– Blessings from God

– Building program confirmed with the presence of God's Shekinah Glory

Compare and contrast this to Nimrod's situation. Note this order:

NIMROD'S BUILDING PROJECT

Foundation of city laid in unity

Visitation from God

Apostolic Intervention – Situation was judged

God disapproves Building Project

– Building program arrested

Confusion of languages instituted

In looking at this scenario, one can see some similarities that Apostolic characteristics may bring, but similarities of characteristics do not yield authenticity.

One definition of Apostle is "sent one." Very clearly in Nimrod's case, one can see that Nimrod did not move into the land of Shinar as a result of God's sending. He began to establish, gather, and build on his own accord and became a world dictator as a result. Dictators are not good examples of who Apostles should be in the earth. His dictatorship gained a measure of power from a secular point of view but that power had no more validity once the Lord intervened in the matter and moved with a corporate anointing to redirect the communication of the unified nation on earth whose goal was to raise it's kingdom to heaven; for Heaven is God's throne and earth is His footstool (Isaiah 66:1). God's feet will not rest in Babylon.

CHAPTER V

ABRAHAM – APOSTOLIC PURSUIT FOR A CITY WITH FOUNDATIONS

Though the nations were dispersed when the building of the tower of Babel was interrupted, a man named Abram yet searched for God in his own manner. Idolatry was extremely prevalent in the lower Mesopotamia region. The city of Ur, known as present day Iraq, served as the headquarters for idol worship. This city flourished with libraries and two-story buildings. A type of air conditioning system existed in Ur as well as a system that provided running water.

The chief god worshipped in Ur was Nanna, who lived at the peak of a claybrick zigguarat. God called Abram out of Ur and "sent" him to a city, which he was unable to identify.

The unique Apostolic characteristic seen here is the sending of a man into a specific region. In this case, it is the son of a prominent businessman, Terah, an idol maker. The son is Abram, meaning, "father of nations."

Abram was instructed by God to separate himself from his territory and his kindred in order to establish a nation from his loins.

Abram was well versed in the celestial sciences, which were prevalent studies in the Chaldeans. Josephus refers to this fact as is mentioned in the "Antiquities of the Jews," Chapter VII. Josephus states, "Berosus mentions our father Abram without naming him, when he says thus:

> *"In the tenth generation after the flood, there was among the Chaldeans a man righteous and great, and skillful in the celestial science."* [8]

Abram recognized through studying the heavenly bodies that the universe does not operate in and of itself, due to the intricate manner in which the universe functioned. God met him during his quest for knowledge regarding the reality of one God.

God called him in the midst of this quest and directed him to another region that he was unfamiliar with, though willing to search for it in obedience.

> *"...he looked for a city which had foundations, whose builder and maker is God." Hebrews 11:10*

Having studied the motion of the stars, moon, sun, and other planets, he recognized an orderly pattern existing, which he believed was operating from the true God's design and origin.

Being intrigued with a search for the God of design and origin, he considered the possibility of the existence of a God who created and maintained principles and precepts. Bob Beckett with Rebecca Wagner-Sytsema in their book Commitment to Conquer state that "Abraham was looking for a city whose foundation – rudimentary principles and precepts – were based on godly principles." [9]

THE SEARCH

1) [10]Canaan – The land of promise, the land of redemption (Red purple dye – from the murex shell), the land of fruitfulness, yet the land of trials.

2) Sichem (Shechem, Sychar) – Place of ill repute, yet place where Abram laid a foundation for prayer by setting aside his first altar to call upon the name of the Lord. This was also the place where Jesus brought Apostolic intervention known as Shecem in Samaria, tearing down traditions of men (John 4). According to Genesis 33:18-20, Jacob came to Shecem, which is located in Canaan and pitched his tent there. He also purchased a parcel of land which presently Jacob's well is believed to be located.

3) Egypt – Egypt represents the old life or the world. It was the place where Abram's trust in God was tested. Abram became fearful for his life because of his wife's beauty. He knew the culture of the Egyptian Pharaoh's and how they respond to beautiful women. Pharaoh took Sarai into his house; God intervened on Abram's behalf and sent judgment to Pharaoh's house in the form of plagues. This forced Pharaoh to release Sarai and dismiss Abram from Egypt.

Apostolic presence in cities can cause kings and queens to take note of their entrance, negotiate with them for exchange of goods and become annoyed with them when God fights their battles.

Abram experienced this with Pharaoh as he searched for a city that was founded on godly principles. Unlike his previous home of Ur, the city with foundations would represent the character of God the Creator. On the other hand, Ur's religious symbol was known as Nanna. Merrill F. Unger believes that Terah, Abram's father, was a worshipper of Ur's god Nanna, not only in Ur, but also in Haran. The city was the first intermittent stop made by his family after leaving Ur on their journey to Haran and eventually Canaan. Unger specifies:

> *"God initially called Abram in Ur, (Acts 7:2-3; Genesis 11:31) and reviewed the call in Haran. He confirmed it in Shechem (12:7), again at Bethel (13:14-17), and twice at Hebron (15:5, 18; 17:1-8), emphasizing how far reaching in importance the call was."*

Unger continues by saying,

> *"It (Haran) was a flourishing city in Abram's day, as it is known from the frequent references to it in Cuneiform sources."* [11]

4) Bethel – dwelling for God or house of God.

Here Abram turned to the spot where he had previously built an altar, at the beginning of his journey. He again recognized Bethel as a place where God's presence may dwell.

Upon leaving Egypt, Abram recognized that this was not the city that he was searching for. The principles were so ungodly that it became necessary for God to send plagues to bring correction. This correction forced the Pharaoh to dismiss Abram and his wife from his premises. Now Abram, after a brief distraction is able to continue his sojourn.

Abram now moves south between Beth-el and Ai, a familiar place where he had initially worshipped God.

For the first time in his sojourn, we see major conflict and a definite enemy, dwelling in the place that is promised to him. The conflict being of an overflow of blessings between Abram and his nephew, Lot. The enemy being, the Canaanite and the Perizzite.

Abram now takes the time to settle the dispute with Lot, for their herdsmen were striving against one another.

> *"And there was strife between the herdsmen of Abram's cattle and the herdsmen of Lot's cattle: and the Canaanite and the Perizzite dwelled then in the land."*
>
> *Genesis 13:7*

Abram's Apostolic intervention caused unresolved issues to surface. Apostles' presence in cities often irritates the status quo, causing persons in leadership in the community to resent their presence. Apostles are able to identify and define trouble spots in regions, mobilizing the saints and equipping them with spiritual warfare tools to bring down strongholds in the regions.

As was the case with Abram, when Lot settled in the area of Sodom and Gomorrah, the stronghold of homosexuality was identified. Though Lot was Abram's nephew, Abram's presence in the region caused this spirit to exemplify itself by vexing Lot. Eventually, the vexation became so great that God responded by communicating with Abram His plans for the region.

The foundation of Sodom and Gomorrah was not a godly one. It's principles and rudiments were base and carnal. Abram served as an Apostolic intercessor in this matter. God's plan was to destroy the region. Abram pleaded with God to spare it by sparing ten righteous people. The number was not found to exist in Sodom and Gomorrah. Abram did not plead for less than ten people, therefore, the twin city was destroyed. Lot and his family were forcibly snatched out before the destruction came. This twin city of Sodom and Gomorrah was destroyed due to its corrupt foundations and principles.

Abram's presence in this region provoked God to deal with this city to disrupt its foundation with brimstone and fire. God, yet remembered His promise to Abram, and Lot was sent out of the region of destruction. Lot sought and found a new dwelling place in the mountains and Abram continued his Apostolic pursuit for a city, which had foundations, a city not made by man.

CHAPTER VI

MOSES – INTERVENER
IN A WILDERNESS

APOSTOLIC ENCOUNTER IN EGYPT

Born in the midst of bondage and oppression under the leadership of an ungodly king, Moses' mother Jochebed, strategically protected his life.

The Israelites had gradually drifted to Egypt from Canaan during the seven (7) years of famine, approximately 2700 BC. They had migrated to Egypt to find substance for survival and remained there for permanent dwelling. This initially worked well for the sons of Jacob and their families. However, the political climate changed through the years, approximately 430, forcing the people to become enslaved in a land, which had originally given them life. This was made possible through the ministry of Joseph, son of Israel, who was promoted above all of his brethren and all of Egypt, except the current Pharaoh. However, as the years passed and Joseph died, the Pharaoh who gave great favor to the Israelites died, and a new ruler emerged on the scene. This ruler was threatened by the intense population increase among the Israelites.

Interestingly enough, Pharaoh employed the Hebrew people to build treasured cities for them. This rulership according to Lawrence O. Richards, occurred around 1730 B.C., Richards states:

> *"Asiatic new comers took over the leadership of lower Egypt, establishing a new dynasty. These rulers known as the Hyksos adopted Egyptian ways. Although relatively few in number, they dominated the administration. It is against this background we understand the ascension of a "new king" who comes to power in Egypt and makes Israel slaves."* 12

This concern resulted in a decree, which ordered the death of all Hebrew male babies at the time of delivery. Israel's enslavement set the stage for God to bring forth a man whom He called to a specific place, for a specific task. This mandate set the stage for a deliverer to come forth. The state was now set for "a sent one" to be commissioned to the nation of Egypt.

Out of the house of Levi came Moses. Moses' mother, Jochebed did not allow him to be thrown into the river as the Pharaoh had decreed. Rather, she strategically prepared an ark for the child to be placed in so that he would be saved in the very river (Nile) that Pharaoh commanded the midwives he employed to use for the destruction of the male Hebrew babies. This is an Apostolic strategy.

Moses' birth brought preparation for an Apostolic setting, as his sister Miriam, the prophetess, assisted in making sure that Moses would be positioned properly and timely in the Nile river for his destiny to be fulfilled, for it was now entrusted within Miriam. His sister, sensitive to the voice of God would be crucial. This demonstrates a type of teamwork with the Apostle/Prophet working together to fulfill a mandate, preceded by an intercessor who assisted in giving birth to a vision – the midwife.

Moses was intercepted by the Pharaoh's daughter (Thermuthis – according to Josephus). Moses was hidden for three months by his parents before he was placed in the Nile River. This aspect of being hidden could be characterized as an Apostolic/Prophetic strategy which respects times and seasons. In Moses' case, he was hidden until the appropriate time for him to be "drawn out of the water." It was then that he was placed in the King's Palace, to be trained by the queen and instructed in Egyptian culture, so that he could at the appointed time apply his understanding to bring deliverance to his nation, which existed within a nation.

As Moses grew up, he began to recognize a strong sensitivity for his destiny. This was demonstrated in an action that was to shape his purpose for the remainder of his life. Observing an Egyptian taskmaster beating one of his brethren, he retaliated by killing the Egyptian. This event catapulted him into his destiny, as he fled to Midian for refuge.

It would be interesting to note here that it was the Midianites who sold Joseph into slavery. This experience placed him in Egypt, which became his training ground originally after the Midianites sold him. Now, Moses finds himself in the country of those who strategically helped him to begin on the journey to his destiny. Joseph's enemies now become Moses support team.

His presence now in the land of Midian, geographically located in the Egyptian Empire, now brings Apostolic intervention. Midian, meaning brawling or contention, emanates immediately the same spirit. As he makes his initial entrance, stopping at a well—this public meeting place was embraced with the presence of seven (7) young ladies, Jethro's daughters, whose responsibility was to water their father's flock.

According to Josephus, Jethro's daughters encountered problems at the well. The land was not well watered; therefore, shepherds would come early to the well to block others from drawing water. The Samaritan woman mentioned in the gospel of St. John encountered Jesus at a well. The time frame appears similar to that of the Midianite women for the purpose of avoiding conflict with other shepherds and their agendas. Josephus states:

> *"For that country having but little water, the Shepherds used to seize on the wells before others came, lest their flocks should want water, and lest it should be spent by others before they came."* [13]

A high level of strife already existed in Midian with the shepherds against the sheepherders, as we can see in this quote from Josephus. The stage is now set for Apostolic intervention. Moses enters into Midian and confronts the Midianite shepherds who were known to have notorious behavior, creating fear where they traveled. This confrontation brought positive change at the well on the day that Moses stopped.

This account at Jethro's well also demonstrates yet another Apostolic attribute. That of being a trail blazer or "a first" to venture into an area or "a

first" to establish a type of order to bring revelatory knowledge regarding scripture and/or plans and purposes of God as well as times and seasons for the church.

Moses dared to step beyond Egyptian tradition to assist and respect shepherdess. Prior to this event, one who was considered to be an Egyptian (Jethro's daughters perceived him as Egyptian) would never assist a shepherd, for this occupation was looked upon with disdain.

To take the shepherding aspect a step further, Moses eventually began to serve as a shepherd in Midian. This was a time of preparation or training for one who had grown up in the king's palace as a prince in the land of Egypt.

Merrill F. Unger confirms the Egyptian perception of shepherding thusly, "Moses as a shepherd, which vocation the Egyptians despised, shared the 'reproach of Christ'" [14] (Hebrews 11:26). This aspect of bearing a reproach can also be translated as being persecuted for the purpose of the kingdom, (experiencing persecution is another strong attribute of an Apostle).

It was in the midst of Moses' ministry to the members of Jethro's tribe and particularly his seven daughters, a type of pastoral ministry, that is to say a ministry to pastors, that God called Moses to a specific people for a specific task for a specific time in history. Apostles are considered as "sent ones." In order to be a sent one, you must receive instruction and direction from God.

Moses was called of God while shepherding Jethro's flock in a desert place or in a wilderness situation. God sovereignly spoke to Moses out of a burning bush. This sight was and is presently considered to be a sign or miracle because the bush burned but was not being consumed. Bushes commonly burned in deserts to the point of being consumed. This experience would now serve as a "signature" of who Moses was and confirm that, He, Jehovah God, the "I Am" sent him.

> *"And God said unto Moses, I AM That I AM: and he said, Thus shalt though say unto the children of Israel, I AM hath sent me unto you."*
> *Exodus 3:14*

Moses was instructed to return to Egypt after 40 years had passed and command Pharaoh to release the Hebrew people that they may go to a new land and worship their God, being Jehovah, The I AM God.

Moses is now expected to operate as a general and as an Apostle through Apostolic intercession, tearing down "Pharaonic" strongholds, (II Corinthians 10:4) interrupting the present status of the Hebrew and the Egyptian government. The Hebrews served (Pharaoh) as excellent builders. Moses had previously served as a Prince in the land. He now returns to the same territory to deliver out a people who are called out by God, who revealed His personal redemptive name Jehovah (Yahweh) to Moses. This is significant in that God reveals who He is according to whom He will be unto us. Now deliverance is needful, therefore, the "delivering God" reveals Himself to the one who will be considered as "the deliverer" for God's people.

Jehovah chooses items commonly seen or used in the wilderness and in the flourishing area of Egypt to demonstrate His power to Moses that Moses will be able to demonstrate God's power to Pharaoh and his magicians.

The plagues represented as one through nine, contested against elements which the Egyptians recognized as gods or holding supernatural powers. The Egyptians were only able to duplicate (counterfeit) two miracles in the form of magic. They were:

1. The plague on the Nile
2. The plague of Frogs

1. Plague on the Nile	6. Plague of Boils
2. Plague of Frogs	7. Plague of Hail
3. Plague of Lice	8. Plague of Locusts
4. Plague of Flies	9. Plague of Darkness
5. Plague of Live Stock	10. Death of Firstborn

"And the Lord did according to the word of Moses; and the frogs died out of the houses, out of the villages, and out of the fields. And they gathered them together upon heaps: and the land stank. But when Pharaoh saw that there was respite, he hardened his heart, and hearkened not unto them; as the Lord had said. And the Lord said unto Moses, Say unto Aaron, Stretch out thy rod, and smite the dust of the land, that it may become lice throughout all the land of Egypt."

Exodus 8:13-16

Although Aaron, Moses' brother, assisted Moses during his intervention against Pharaoh, Moses was the Apostolic presence that God used to bring Israel out of Egypt.

This Pharaoh is now defeated, Amenhotep II, a 22 year old ruler. This encounter that Moses experienced with Pharaoh was due to a conflict over objects and places of worship.

Moses had requested leave for the Israelites in order to worship Jehovah God in the wilderness.

Amenhotep II was unable to comprehend the need to worship a "god" who appears to be neither visible and did not seem to protect his people from the bondage of slavery. Therefore, the reigning Pharaoh mocked Moses' request to exodus the nation of Israel.

Pharaoh (Amenhotep II) refused this request, forcing the hand of God to use Moses to demonstrate "Apostolic signs and wonders."

This demonstration as stated earlier, proved that the God of Moses reigns above all gods. Moses stood fast in his conviction, knowing that he had a mandate to deliver the children of Israel out of Egyptian bondage into the wilderness for a worship experience required by Jehovah-God.

Taking the children of Israel into the wilderness to worship establishes a challenging order of worship as an Apostolic venture.

Initially, the Pharaoh insisted that the men be released to serve God, Jehovah *(Exodus 10:8)*. This was not God's plan or order for worship. It has always been God's plan for the entire family to worship Him together. He even allows for the release of their possessions, which coincides with the act of worship when one offers their substance as well as themselves unto God, as we worship.

"And Moses said, We will go with our young and with our old, with our sons and with our daughters, with our flocks and with our herds will we go; for we must hold a feast unto the Lord."

Exodus 10:9

The conflict regarding worship should not be viewed lightly. Moses was in contest as an intervener with Pharaoh who was opposed to worship of Jehovah by the Hebrew people. In addition, Moses needed to be able to offer sacrifices to Jehovah God rather than Pharaoh.

This gesture aggravated the scenario even more, for worship is not complete without an offering. Moses specifically makes this clear by requesting sacrifices and burnt offerings. Moses was even specific with the Hebrew people as to which animal would be sacrificed for the offering. The lamb was selected, which points to Jesus the "Lamb of God," slain before the foundation of the world.

Moses established an order of worship for the Hebrew nation that will be remembered and implemented for generations to come.

"And this day shall be unto you for a memorial; and ye shall keep it a feast to the Lord throughout your generations; ye shall keep it a feast by an ordinance for ever."

Exodus 12:14

Following much conflict with Pharaoh after the children of Israel slew the Lambs and performed their final ceremonies in the land of Egypt, they journeyed.

They journeyed, but not without incident. As the camp of Hebrew people mixed with many other nations, moved out of Egypt, the Pharaoh tried to hinder them, which is typical of the struggle that one may face when determining to worship God. Pharaoh's heart became hardened after the exodus began. He then decided to pursue after the Hebrews, which forced Moses to draw upon God for a miraculous delivery. The army was behind them and a sea before them. Apostolic intervention is necessary once again in the wilderness of Egypt.

Moses inquired of God and God instructed him to stretch his hand and the waters of the Red Sea parted. This can be considered as a wonder as the term "miracle" was not used in the Old Testament. On the other hand, "wonder" is used in both the old and New Testament.

"And I will stretch out my hand, and smite Egypt with all my wonders which I will do in the midst thereof: and after that he will let you go."

Exodus 3:20

"Who is like unto thee, O Lord, among the gods? Who is like thee, glorious in holiness, fearful in praises, doing wonders?"

Exodus 15:11

"And there appeared a great wonder in heaven; a woman clothed with the sun, and the moon under her feet, and upon her head a crown of twelve stars."

Revelations 12:1

As the waters parted, the children of Israel marched, processed onward on dry land. The man, Moses whose name means drawn out of water or "Moiises," a person who is preserved out of the water; for the Egyptians call water "Moii." [15] Moses is delivered from destruction by water. His destiny was to bring a great people out of bondage in a wilderness, toward a land where worship could be realized.

CHAPTER VII

NEHEMIAH – GOVERNMENTAL INTERVENTION

Nehemiah was a governmental official who served King Artaxerxes in Susa (Shushan), approximately 444 BC. His skills in business management were absolutely crucial during a time when the nation of Israel needed their homeland rebuilt.

God strategically placed Nehemiah in a high profile environment so that restoration of the temple in Jerusalem could be realized through his Apostolic direction and implementation in the city.

When Nehemiah learned that many of his brethren were in affliction in Jerusalem and that the status of the city was that of anarchy, he sought a plan to bring change to the situation.

Having been a faithful staff member in the King's court, he immediately gained favor with King Artaxerxes regarding his home and received a mandate to go and rebuild what had been torn down. King Artaxerxes sent Nehemiah to Jerusalem for the specific purpose of restoring the city of his homeland.

Presently, Nehemiah resided in Shushan, located approximately 150 miles north of what we presently know as the Persian Gulf. While living in this resort area or winter haven for kings, Nehemiah received word from one of his brethren, Hanani, of the great distress prevailing in Jerusalem.

The walls were broken down and they had been burned with fire. The city was now totally vulnerable to attack. The walls represented protection and strength and the gates reflected assurance to its citizens that the authority of eldership was in place. Walls also indicated that someone would be stationed at the gate to note entrance and exits, which would certainly monitor activity of strangers approaching the city's gates.

Nehemiah received special appointment from his superior, King Artaxerxes to return to Jerusalem to bring restoration. Note the following Apostolic aspects in the life of Nehemiah:

SENT ONE

"And the king said unto me, (the queen also sitting by him,) For how long shall thy journey be? And when wilt thou return? So it pleased the king to send me; and I set him a time."

Nehemiah 2:6

Apostolic intervention within cities cannot be truly Apostolic unless one is divinely sent for purpose. Nehemiah was sent to the city of Jerusalem to assess damages suffered while the inhabitants had been in captivity.

POSSESS GREAT FAVOR

"...So it pleased the king to send me; and I set him a time. Moreover I said unto the king, If it please the king, let letters be given me to the governors beyond the river, that they may convey me over till I come into Judah."

Nehemiah 2:6b-7

Apostles must be in position to move in and out of adverse circumstances without being hindered or delayed by a lack of resources and manpower. It is pertinent that they receive favor from God and man.

When Nehemiah received the mandate to go to Jerusalem to intervene in the desolation matter of the city, he also was given letters to present to the governors of each region for passage.

These papers were issued because of *"the good hand of my God upon me"* (Nehemiah 2:8). Nehemiah also received additional favor from the king, as he sent captains of the army and horsemen with him.

STRATEGIST

Apostles are men and women who understand the necessity, power, and wisdom of strategy, as Nehemiah.

As he moved discreetly, upon arriving in Jerusalem he quickly determined what may hinder his journey. He recognized that it would not be wise to take too many people with him to spy out Jerusalem. He also discerned that night travel would be safer and more effective initially.

Relating to methods of travel, Nehemiah assessed the accessibility of some of the places that he needed to travel and decided that he would have to travel to some extent on foot.

Nehemiah applied the wisdom of practicing silence prior to executing a mission. He did not speak to anyone regarding what his mission was in Jerusalem, neither the Jews, the priests, the nobles, the officials, nor any others who were involved.

When the time was good, Nehemiah reviewed with his assistants, traveling companions and potential workers, his plan. He was going to bring an Apostolic dimension to Jerusalem. Restoration was on the horizon.

CIVIL ORDER INSTITUTED

Nehemiah specifically designed a plan, which we will designate as civil order. This civil order would take him from assessing the damages done to Jerusalem to appointing individuals for positions regarding worship and revival.

The civil order consisted of fourteen (14) steps or directives observed and implemented by Nehemiah. They are as follows:

NEHEMIAH'S CIVIL ORDER

1) Assess the damage done by the fire.
2) Institution of Prayer/Praise to fortify against ridicule of enemy (Nehemiah 2:19-20).
3) Set order for positioning of each builder (Nehemiah 3).
4) Repeating Prayer/Praise for fortification (Nehemiah 4:4-5).

5) Establishment of armory for protection (Nehemiah 4:13-17).
6) Warfare praise established (Nehemiah 4:18-21).
7) Body guards established.
8) Assess debts and reestablished order for credit, buying, and selling produce and land (Nehemiah 5:1-13).
9) Prophetic demonstration to confirm restoration of land and produce (Nehemiah 5:13).
10) Governmental authority reconfirmed (Nehemiah 5:14-18).
11) Intercessors sent to stop the enemy's voice.
12) Set governors in charge of Jerusalem including instructions for watchmen on the wall (Nehemiah 6).
13) Establishes accountability (Nehemiah 7:5).
14) Solemn assembly restored – New beginning (Nehemiah 8:12).

Taking a close look at some of the fourteen directives, we can see consistencies and characteristics of Apostolic intervention. Specifically, we see represented:

1) **Boldness**
To enter into a city and make quality decisions in the midst of disaster. As Nehemiah observed the ruins of the gates, he was cognizant that strength, authority, and leadership were minimized in the city and that his presence, which brought "an Apostolic authority" could bring change to a situation which appeared hopeless.

2) **Prayer and Praise**
Vital aspects of Apostolic ministry. A city, which does not engage in spiritual warfare through the vehicle of prayer and praise, is a powerless city. Prayer opens the channel to communicate with God through Jesus who is now the Christ. During Nehemiah's day, Jesus was often known as the Lord God (Hebrew).
Prayer provides opportunity to identify and pull down strong holds over regions.
Praise lays a foundation for prayer to go forth. It pushes principalities, chief ruling spirits, and the powers of darkness out of the pathway that is needed for the answer to flow to the region and it allows for angels to be assigned to do war in the heavenlies on behalf of those praying.
Apostles can make a great impact upon cities in their region by establishing prayer networks or companies to bombard the forces of the enemy. Through the implementation of praise and worship warfare can change the atmosphere in the area.
Nehemiah understood the power of prayer and praise.

3) **Laying foundations**
Building programs or plans require order and a systemized plan. Each builder must know the blueprint and the guidelines.

Eliashib, the high priest rose up first to build on behalf of the people. The priest set the example for the congregation as they begin the building process. After Nehemiah activated the congregation to rebuild. Following Eliashib's example were many other teams such as the men of Jericho, the nobles, Gibeon, the goldsmiths', and rulers of various parts of Jerusalem.

4) <u>**Establishing A Watch For The Protection Of Workers**</u>

The enemy often mocked the Nehemiah project by speaking words of defeat and projecting fear. This did not affect the project, adversely, it enhanced it. These words of mockery boasted Nehemiah and the builders to work toward their goal even the more.

Upon realizing that the enemy's forces were increased against the congregation, Nehemiah established an army of watchman to protect the work.

The mockery was carried out to such an extent as to delay progress of the building project, by encouraging Nehemiah to cease work upon the wall and attend a meeting in the valley of Ono with Sanballat, the governor of Samaria, Tobiah, the Ammonite, and Geshem, the Arab.

Nehemiah decided to meet with his opponents at this seacoast village. This was truly applied wisdom on his part, for the enemy now sought to deter the rebuilding project of the walls and gates of the city of Jerusalem by indirect warfare.

Apostolic ministry is considered as warfare or an Apostolic career (II Corinthians 10:4) (Greek word strateia for warfare); therefore, it is important for Apostles to maintain focus to implement and maintain clear direction for the mandate.

Nehemiah was given a mandate. This mandate was that of rebuilding broken walls and gates. Walls represent and give support, strengthen and protect. Gates represents a specified place where authority is developed and maintained in a city. Guards must be raised up and trained to watch over the gates of a city. Leaders must be appointed and anointed to stand guard at gates to know who can and cannot enter or exit.

Intercessors must be brought forth into the kingdom of God to pray at the gates of their cities to declare God's grace, mercy, and protection for a city.

Upon completion of the project Nehemiah gave the charge to his brother, Hanani, which means "gracious" and Hananiah, which means the leader of the citadel to watch over Jerusalem.

Nehemiah delivered the following instructions to Hanani and Hananiah.

"Do not let the gates of Jerusalem be opened until the sun is hot; and while they stand guard, let them shut and bar the doors; and appoint guards from among the inhabitants of Jerusalem, one at his watch station, and another in front of his own house."

Nehemiah 7:3

Following the appointment of Hanani and Hananiah to be the keepers of Jerusalem, Nehemiah developed a census program to determine which families would reside in the city.

The total number to reside was expected to be 42,360.

Nehemiah, who began serving as the King's Cupbearer, became a statesman and was later appointed governor. A governor, who re-established the city of Jerusalem, always recognized that the Lord's hand was good upon him.

CHAPTER VIII

APOSTLES – INTERRUPTING RELIGIOUS AND ECONOMIC SYSTEMS

As the foundation of the early church was being established, the Apostles, which had been called and appointed by Jesus of Nazareth, the Son of the Living God, moved sovereignly from village to village and city to city intervening against the "status quo," changing religious systems and interrupting economic forecasts.

The following Apostolic interventions are presented to give us a glimpse of what we can expect during the 21st century as the Apostolic prophets, Apostolic pastors, Apostolic evangelists, and Apostolic teachers emerge.

Mark 5:1-20
Chief Apostle: Jesus Christ of Nazareth
City: Gadara
System Interrupted: Economic

After crossing the Sea of Galilee and landing on the shores of Gadara (Gergesne), Jesus was met by a demon-possessed man whose name was legion, meaning many.[16] The man, driven by demons ran to worship Jesus and the demons bargained with Jesus to remain in their assigned location, the perimeter of the sea in Galilee and reached a compromise to enter into the swine.

When Jesus commanded the demons to come out of the man, they immediately obeyed and at the same time were permitted to enter into the swine. The swine ran violently downhill into the sea, perishing as they traveled.

While the demons, about 6,000, were satisfied to remain in the region, the merchants were devastated because their economy collapsed as a result of the powerful words spoken by a stranger in their village. Immediately, the merchants began to ask him to leave the area. Jesus' presence and authority had cost the merchants 2,000 swine at $35.00 each, for a total on today's market of $70,000.00.

The businessmen were annoyed but the man who had been demon possessed was free and prepared to be discipled by Jesus, (Mark 5:15) but He encouraged the man to go and share the good news (Mark 5:18-20). As a result of the man's proclamation, ten cities were impacted and made aware of the miracle working power of Jesus in Gadara.

Acts 10
Apostle: Peter
City: Joppa and Caesarea (Capital of Judea)
Systems Interrupted: Religious

A gentile whose name was Cornelius, experienced a visitation from God (an Angel of God) in a vision. The scripture specifies that this event occurred about the ninth hour. This would have placed the event at about 3:00 p.m. This is important so as to understand that Cornelius would most likely have been awake at this time of the day. If an individual has a vision while sleeping, sometimes the credibility is lessened.

In addition, his integrity as a centurion, one who has authority over a regiment, gives credibility to his testimony. The scriptures give a colorful description of the event. Note the following passage:

> *"And when he looked on him, he was afraid, and said, What is it, Lord? And he said unto him, Thy prayers and thine alms are come up for a memorial before God. And now send men to Joppa, and call for one Simon whose surname is Peter: He lodgeth with one Simon a tanner, whose house is by the sea side: he shall tell thee what thou oughtest to do."*
>
> *Acts 10: 4-6*

Cornelius immediately responded to the words from the Angel of God and followed the instructions given to him to send men to Joppa and inquire of Simon Peter, who was lodging at the home of Simon, the tanner.

At the same time, God was preparing Simon Peter for an event that would turn the helm of the Christian community. Peter went up on the housetop to pray about noontime. God was now able to use the lunch hour as a strategic time to dismiss racial prejudices that Peter held regarding the gentile nation.

A sheet was released out of heaven, which carried various kinds of animals, beasts, creeping things and birds of the air (Acts 10:10-12).

The voice of the Lord commanded Peter to kill and eat. Peter responded adamantly to the voice that he would not eat due to the uncleanness of the items being presented. The Lord corrected Peter's previous mindset so that he would understand that what he knew as clean or unclean no longer had the same significance. Peter was not aware that God could and does clean what we have known and comprehended to be unclean.

As Peter accepted this revelation, three men stood outside to speak with him. They had come by instruction of Cornelius, their master. He directed them to the house of the tanner, where Peter lodged, that he may invite him to Caesarea to proclaim the Word of the Lord.

Common knowledge existed among the Jewish people that a Jewish person was forbidden to enter into the home of a gentile. In addition, fellowship at a meal was equally revoking.

Prior to traveling to Caesarea, a seaport region, frequently where "the scene of disturbances vs. cities of mixed Jewish-Gentile population tended to be," [17] Peter invited the men into the home of Simon the tanner. The home was located in Joppa, a city located on the Mediterranean Sea, close to Jerusalem.

The next day a delegation from Joppa traveled with Peter to visit the home of Cornelius, guided by the three men who served Peter with an invitation.

Peter, being greeted by Cornelius the following day, explained that his visit was not common but in obedience to the voice of God, accepted the hospitality and determined to share the gospel with Cornelius and the entire household of friends and family. During Peter's preaching, the Holy Spirit fell on the people gathered. The Holy Spirit confirmed the truth of Peter's words.

This event truly disrupted the present theology of the Hebrew nation. The religious system which embraced racial and theological ideals was overthrown, for a Jewish preacher had entered the home of a gentile and declared the gospel to individuals who were not only considered unclean but also uncircumcised. These "uncircumcised gentiles," also began to speak with tongues, give God praise and experience water baptism as an outward expression of a very special new work.

The religious leaders in Judea—a derivative of the word "Jewish"—were displeased with Peter. His decision to evangelize among persons, who were not or would not become Jews, was repulsive to them. He did not hesitate to explain how God had interrupted even his prayer time to reveal that the gentiles should not be called common or unclean. Peter concluded that he could not withstand what God had determined as acceptable. Convicted, after hearing Peter's message (Acts 10:34-43), the Apostles and brethren who had contended (sharply disagreed) with Peter accepted the Gentiles as believers.

ACTS 16:16-24
Apostle: Paul/Silas
City: Philippi
Systems Interrupted: Religious and Economic

During Paul's Apostolic travels to the region of Macedonia, he sailed to an area known as Philippi, a commercial center in Macedonia. Macedonia is a country north of Greece.

Paul, along with Timothy and Silas, traveled to Macedonia in response to a specific call for help that he received in a vision.

> *"And a vision appeared to Paul in the night; There stood a man of Macedonia, and prayed him, saying, Come over into Macedonia, and help us."*
>
> *Acts 16:9*

Having immediately set sail to Macedonia from Troas, upon arriving, they spent several days in the region prior to locating a synagogue. There was apparently not a synagogue in the area. According to Ronald F. Youngblood:

> *"...the city did not have the necessary number of Jewish males (ten) to form a synagogue, because Paul met with a group of women for prayer outside the city gate."* [18]
>
> *Acts 16:13*

Among the women was a businesswoman who was a seller of purple (expensive dye) whose name was Lydia. She became Paul's first European convert. After Paul baptized her and her household, he and his traveling companions were invited to stay in her home. Here a church was founded.

On one occasion when Paul, Silas, and Timothy went to prayer, a slave girl who was a diviner met them and began to cry out.

> *"The same followed Paul and us, and cried, saying, These men are the servants of the most high God, which shew unto us the way of salvation."*
>
> *Acts 16:17 NKJV*

> *"This girl followed Paul and the rest of us, shouting, "These men are servants of the Most High God, who are telling you the way to be saved."*
>
> *Acts 16:17 NIV*

The spirit of divination was not an acceptable source to proclaim or affirm the status and ministry of Paul and his companions in this new region. The city of Philippi was a foremost city in Macedonia, which allowed great potential for church growth. The Egnatian way, the main overland route between Asia and West, ran through Philippi. This city was a cultural art and sports center as well as a religious focal point, which boasted two large temples.

Paul allowed the slave girl to follow him for many days, however, this was not allowed to continue, as Paul commanded the spirit of divination to come out of her because her statement could have brought confusion to possible new converts. Paul needed to have absolutely no association or fellowship, which could have appeared to be paganism. According to a reference in the Quest Study Bible, "Pagan religions of the day commonly referred to a most high god, who was just one of their many gods." [19] Fortune telling was her occupation, which brought her master a great income. The Apostle Paul's reaction to this slave girl caused uproar in the city. Her owner's income would now begin to decline; therefore they seized Paul and Silas and dragged them into the market place to face the authorities.

As the authorities of Philippi were consulted, economy did not seem to be the issue, though this was the main problem. Apparently, the owners of the slave girl felt that they could get some degree of justice if the case were

to be presented on a religious/governmental level. Their argument had set out to induce a riot in the city; however, a riot developed but it broke forth as a result of deception. Paul and Silas were presented as Jews coming into the city to cause trouble.

As a result, they were beaten and thrown in jail. This decision proved to be good for three reasons:

1) Paul and Silas were able to evangelize in jail and birth additional converts.

2) The power of Praise and Worship could be presented as a weapon of warfare, as a great earthquake occurred as Paul and Silas began to magnify God and everyone was set free.

3) The Roman magistrates who were led to believe that the Apostles were interrupting their religious practices had to apologize to them and release them, though their very presence did defy their religious practices and upset the economy of some of their business.

CHAPTER IX

THE JEDAH COMPANY – WOMEN BUILDING WITH NETWORK FOCUS

The book of Proverbs refers to a group of women who would, as a company, publish the gospel. A company could be considered as a group of ten or more persons with network focus.

Though distinct in function and distant in years, yet networking in purpose, this chapter will feature women in the Bible who had similar calls, appointments, and focus. They are Junia, Esther, Deborah, Abigail, and Huldah. They are not listed in order of appearance in the scriptures but their order yields a beautiful acronym, JEDAH.

JUNIA

ESTHER

DEBORAH

ABIGAL

HULDAH

The women listed above, all demonstrated Apostolic attributes. Junia, an Apostle of note, highly respected by Paul, the Apostle. Esther, a queen/general, who came to the kingdom to save a nation. Deborah, a prophetess/judge, who led the nation of Israel in subsequent years. Abigail, the wife of Nabal, a prophetic intercessor, who diverted a war with wisdom and intercession, and finally Huldah, a prophetess/teacher, whose ability to interpret scripture with boldness and send the word of the Lord to the Judean King (Josiah) whose reign was redirected by Huldah's instructions and prophetic direction.

JUNIA FOCUS:
TO STRENGTHEN APOSTLES
CITY: ROME

"Salute Andronicus and Junia, my kinsmen, and my fellow prisoners, who are of note among the Apostles, who also were in Christ before me."
Romans 16:7

The book of Romans introduces and identifies Junia. Junia's Apostolic role impacted Rome.

The last chapter of the book of Romans happens to be one of commendation, salutations, and a few last minute instructions for the Roman church (Romans 16).

One of the persons to whom greetings were sent was Junia. She is referred to by Paul along with Andronicus. The two are considered as countrymen and fellow prisoners who were of note among the Apostles and laborers who ministered before Paul's ministry time (Romans 16:7).

Many argue that Junia was not a female since Paul refers to the persons as countrymen. According to Trombley's research, both names "Andronicus and Junian are in the accusative case." [20] He states further that when uncertainty exist, it is best to consult writings of the early church fathers, note the following quotes of early church fathers:

> *"Oh, how great is the devotion of this woman that she should be counted worthy of the appellation of an Apostle!"*

Origin of Alexandria (c. 185-253) – "The name was a variant of Julia."

Trombley further argues: "What would Junia have been doing in prison with Paul if she was a confined, quiet lady." [21] Apostles were often thrown into prison because of their beliefs and strong preaching, which challenged the status quo of the city government.

In addition to Trombley's research, Freida C. White, quotes Theophylact, a Greek, regarding Junia's greatness, saying:

> *"Furthermore the greatness exists because they are Apostles, but especially in the company of a woman, Junia, much unity. It is more great, because they were so distinguished. Furthermore they were distinguished in fact by their works."* [22]

The Grecian reference to Junia continues to confirm feminine gender for Junia as well as Apostolic position. It appears that her Apostolic ministry brought strength to Paul in prison in Rome, as well as strength to Andronicus, her kindred.

A MacArthur Study Bible reference declares:

> *"Perhaps a married couple," since 'Junia' can be a woman's name. 'Fellow prisoners,' is probably a reference to their actually sharing the same cell or adjacent cells at some point. 'Note among the Apostles,' their ministry with Paul, and perhaps with Peter and some of the other Apostles in Jerusalem before Paul was converted, was well known and appreciated by the Apostles."* [23]

ESTHER FOCUS:
TO SAVE A NATION
CITY: SUSA (SHUSHAN)

> *"For if thou altogether holdest thy peace at this time, then shall their enlargement and deliverance arise to the Jews from another place; but thou and thy father's house shall be destroyed: and who knoweth whether thou art come to the kingdom for such a time as this?"*
>
> *Esther 4:14*

The city which Esther, the Queen of Persia impacted was Susa (Shushan). An ancient city situated in what is known as ancient Persia, approximately 200 miles East of Babylon. This city served as a winter resort and capital for kings.

In this setting, Esther emerged with a network focus to counteract the destruction of her people.

Esther, a Hebrew orphan, was among the exiled in Persia who had been earlier carried into captivity in Babylon. Remaining in Persia proved to be a divine decision.

Esther's (Jewish for Hadassah) uncle Mordecai raised her as his own daughter after the death of her mother and father.

Having chosen to remain in Persia rather than return to Jerusalem was a decision, which would share the destiny of not only Esther and Mordecai, but the destiny of the Jewish nation.

These exiles lived under the authority of King Ahasuerus, also considered as XERXES I (486-465 BC). His Kingdom extended from India to Ethiopia. In the third year of his reign, he began a lengthy celebration, which lasted for a six-month period. The celebration placed him in a merry making mood. During this episode, the current queen, Vashti, was requested to come before King Ahauserus. The custom in Persia regarding banquets was to hold the men and women's banquets separately (Esther 1:9).

The king's request for Vashti to present herself at his banquet would require her to defy the law of the land, which even the king was expected to adhere. The law had been established to protect the women from indecent behavior as it relates to male guest. She chose to deny the king's request, apparently to maintain dignity. This resulted in having her crown transferred to another.

Eventually, a new queen was selected after a lengthy search throughout the Persian Kingdom. Esther, the Jewish orphan, was selected. This selection served as a divine intervention for the Jewish nation, when Esther came to the kingdom, the Jewish people were on the brink of being annihilated by Haman, a high court official. This discontentment rested in his insecurity regarding Mordecai, her adopted father, who was a court official of a lower rank. However, Haman did not feel that Mordecai respected him, so his anger ruled him. He planned to also assassinate the king. As this information was revealed to Esther, her destiny became clear. God could now use her position as Queen and her beauty and wisdom to bring about Apostolic intervention. Though in exile from her native country, her presence in Susa positioned her to focus on a regional need. Esther fasted and prayed for favor to intercede or intervene for her people. Favor was granted after she received counsel from Mordecai, that she *"perhaps was brought to the Kingdom for such a time as this."* (Esther 4:14)

After favor was granted from the king, she petitioned him to save his people. Her wish was more than granted. She was offered as much as half of the kingdom. A woman who came from obscurity was now standing before a king. Esther was a sent woman who was destined to speak to the highest earthly official of the land and see a nation within a nation freed from death and ushered into a new level of living.

As a result of this event, a feast has been established in the Jewish nation, which is called Purim. This feast day is celebrated on the 14th or 15th day of Adar, the twelfth month (Feb – March).

Esther's willingness to network with Mordecai and the king brought great results for the Jewish people. She represented them exceedingly well.

DEBORAH FOCUS:
COUNSEL AND EXHORT
GOVERNMENTAL OFFICIALS
CITY: RAMAH AND BETHEL

The name Deborah means "bee," indicative of one who is industrious and productive. Deborah was both. Her natural focus was that of bringing a community together to address issues, solve them, and strengthen leadership for battle against the Canaanite oppressions.

Deborah's mandate was that of judging the people as disputes arose or major decisions needed to be addressed. Her region consisted of Ramah and Bethel. Ramah was the home of the prophet Samuel. It was also a prominent place during the reign of the kings. It means high place. This is where watchmen guarded the land. It was located five miles north of Jerusalem.

Bethel, means house of God. It is located ten miles north of Jerusalem. Deborah's place of ministry was located between the two cities north of Jerusalem.

Her presence under the palm tree brought stability to the region, having God's prophetess present to discuss and solve matters.

One of the greater matters of the land dealt with challenging Barak, general of the army of Israel, to obey the mandate that the Lord had given him, saying:

> *"...Hath not the Lord God of Israel commanded, saying go and draw toward mount Tabor, and take with thee ten thousand men of the children of Naphtali and of the children of Zebulun?"*
>
> *Judges 4:6b*

Upon hearing the word of the prophetess Deborah, Barak agreed to obey the word of the Lord contingent upon Deborah going to battle with him. She, however, explained to Barak that the Lord would not honor him in battle with the final victory, but it would be given to a woman.

Barak went up to battle with Deborah, his hosts of ten thousand men, to Kadesh and experienced great exploits.

The Lord had given Barak a strategy that would yield a victory when spoken through Deborah to challenge him to go up and fight the battle. Specifically, the prophetic direction for strategic warfare was that He would "draw Barak into the river Kishon and deliver them into his hands for battle." However, Sisera was told that Barak had gone up before him, therefore, he went up with his nine hundred chariots of iron and his host of people from Harosheth to the river Kishon. This river rises at the foot of Mount Tabor and winds through the plain of Jezereel. When it rains, this plain becomes extremely muddy, causing difficulty for chariots to travel.

> *"Lord, when thou wentest out of Seir, when thou marchedst out of the field of Edom, the earth trembled, and the heavens dropped, the clouds also dropped water."*
>
> *Judges 5:4*

This is where the great battle took place. All men were slain in Jabin's army and Sisera, the captain, fled on foot.

He ran into the tent of Jael, the wife of Heber the Kenites. He felt safe because of a peace agreement between Jabin of Hazor and Heber the Kenite. On the other hand, the prophetess had revealed the plan of God to Barak, that when He sent him out to battle, that the honor would be bestowed upon a woman. The woman, Jael, had positioned herself to receive Sisera.

As she set the atmosphere for him to rest, in the midst of deep sleep, she drove a nail into his temple. During this time, when Barak was yet seeking Sisera, it was important to destroy the captains of armies in battle or the kings of nations. Destroying the head of a nation was necessary to declare total victory. The captain was destroyed, but the honor was given to Jael, a woman bold and brave enough to use a domestic strategy to win a military battle. Deborah demonstrated Apostolic characteristics as she led the nation of Israel into a glorious time of peace, after many years of Canaanite oppression. Her wisdom, counsel, and military strategies brought rest for a long season to a turbulent nation. She was the first judge to be known also as a prophet. She sang prophetic-poetic warfare songs, prior to the 20th and the 21st Century. Deborah did great exploits as a prophetic judge and an Apostolic general. Village life had ceased in Israel until Deborah arose as a mother in Israel.

> *"And the hand of the children of Israel prospered, and prevailed against Jabin the king of Canaan, until they had destroyed Jabin king of Canaan."*
> *Judges 4:24*

Deborah and Barak sang a song about the battle and it's victory, *"And the land had rest forty years."* (Judges 5:31b)

ABIGAIL FOCUS:
DIVERT WAR BETWEEN DAVID
AND NABAL AT CARMEL

CITY: CARMEL

Located in a small village approximately two miles north of Maon, his home lay in Carmel, the business location of Nabal, a very prosperous man.

Nabal had made previous arrangements with David to distribute food to his men in exchange for David's men offering protection for Nabal's prosperity. When David camped in the wilderness of Paran, following the death of the prophet Samuel, he sent out ten men to require provisions from Nabal, located a few miles away.

Though "Carmel" means fruitful field, Nabal (foolish) refused to send food to David, pretending not to know who David was, nor recall his commitment.

"...Behold, David sent messengers out of the wilderness to salute our master; and he railed on them. But the men were very good unto us, and we were not hurt, neither missed we any thing, as long as we were conversant with them, when we were in the fields: They were a wall unto us both by night and day, all the while we were with them keeping the sheep."

I Samuel 25:14b-16

On the other hand, when Nabal's wife, Abigail, a woman of good understanding, a woman of wisdom and ability to give wise counsel, heard how rude Nabal had been to David's men, she took charge.

One of Nabal's men thought it wise to inform Abigail of certain impending danger:

"But one of the young men told Abigail, Nabal's wife, saying, Behold, David sent messengers out of the wilderness to salute our master; and he railed on them."

I Samuel 25:14

"Now therefore know and consider what thou wilt do; for evil is determined against our master, and against all his household: for he is such a son of Belial, that a man cannot speak to him."

I Samuel 25:17

Abigail quickly began to prepare provisions for David and his legion, moving into Apostolic distinction. The supplies consisted of two hundred loaves, two bottles of wine, five sheep already dressed, five measures of parched corn, one hundred clusters of raisins, and two hundred cakes of figs.

Her ability to assess a matter, think and move quickly was Apostolic. Apostles understand times, seasons, leaders of nations and regions, and warfare. Abigail's sensitivity to these aspects was crucial to the situation.

As she lighted off her donkey and fell at David's feet on her face, she demonstrated that she understood how to present herself before governmental authorities in her region. She also understood that worship is a form of warfare, which she displayed before David. According to II Corinthians 10:4a, *"...the weapons of our warfare (strateia – Greek) are not carnal."* Greek translation = Apostolic career.

Worship is a dynamic weapon of warfare. Worship consists of yielding, submitting, and giving. Abigail brought an abundant offering to David. She also pointed to what would later be considered in New Testament terminology as "Apostolic distribution." (Acts 4:35)

Abigail also demonstrated the power of Apostolic-prophetic intercession as she served as the one to stand in the gap for the city of Maon and Carmel, by advising David not to declare war.

"Now therefore, my lord, as the Lord liveth, and as thy soul liveth, seeing the Lord hath withholden thee from coming to shed blood, and from avenging thyself with thine own hand, now let thine enemies, and they that seek evil to my lord, be as Nabal. And now this blessing which thine handmaid hath

brought unto my lord, let it even be given unto the young men that follow my lord. I pray thee, forgive the trespass of thine handmaid: for the Lord will certainly make my lord a sure house; because my lord fighteth the battles of the Lord, and evil hath not been found in thee all thy days."

I Samuel 25:26-28

She spoke prophetic words of national meaning to David declaring:

"And it shall come to pass when the Lord shall have done to my lord according to all the good that he hath spoken concerning thee, and shall have spoken concerning thee, and shall have appointed thee ruler over Israel; That this shall be no grief unto thee, nor offense of heart unto my lord, either that thou hast shed blood causeless, or that my lord hath avenged himself: but when the Lord shall have dealt well with my lord, then remember thine handmaid."

I Samuel 25:30-31

David received Abigail's counsel and arrested any plans that he had to destroy Nabal and his household. Abigail had referred to David in her plea to him as her Lord and as his handmaiden. It came to pass that Nabal learned what had transpired after returning to Maon—he died—And David sent for Abigail who made haste and took five damsels with her and became David's wife.

HULDAH FOCUS:
INTERPRET SCRIPTURES AND
PROPHESY TO NATIONAL LEADERS

CITY: JERUSALEM

The city of Jerusalem was the setting for Huldah, the prophetess' headquarters. The wife of Shallum, Keeper of the Wardrobe, Huldah was a contemporary of Jeremiah and Zephaniah.

According to Josephus, she dwelt at the college in Jerusalem. Some commentators argue that college in this context refers to "quarters" complex or suburbs. On the other hand, she could very well have been a professor at a school for prophets as Elijah mentored prophets in the school for prophets.

When King Josiah instructed the scribe to go to the high priest to determine the status of the treasury for the Lord's house, the high priest announced that he had found the book of the law. (II Kings 22: 4-8)

This book of the law convicted Josiah, Judah's young king to study the law, receive interpretation and carry out what the law stated. This find took place while the temple was being repaired and restored. Josiah's conviction caused him to tear his garment upon hearing the reading of God's word. This level of repentance prompted him to desire to have a deeper understanding of what was being declared in the word. Josiah determined that representatives should be sent to Huldah, the prophetess in Jerusalem, in the chief city, Palestine, and often noted to mean "Salem," interpreted peace.

Huldah read and interpreted the law for the delegation from the King's house. Huldah prophesied:

> *"And she said unto them, Thus saith the Lord God of Israel, Tell the man that sent you to me, Thus saith the Lord, Behold, I will bring evil upon this place, and upon the inhabitants thereof, even all the words of the book which the king of Judah hath read: Because they have forsaken me, and have burned incense unto other gods, that they might provoke me to anger with all the works of their hands; therefore my wrath shall be kindled against this place, and shall not be quenched. But to the king of Judah which sent you to enquire of the Lord, thus shall ye say to him, Thus saith the Lord God of Israel, As touching the words which thou hast heard; Because thine heart was tender, and thou hast humbled thyself before the Lord, when thou heardest what I spake against this place, and against the inhabitants thereof, that they should become a desolation and a curse, and hast rent thy clothes, and wept before me; I also have heard thee, saith the Lord. Behold therefore, I will gather thee unto thy fathers, and thou shalt be gathered into thy grave in peace; and thine eyes shall not see all the evil which I will bring upon this place. And they brought the king word again."*
>
> *II Kings 23:15-20*

Huldah's prophetic words were Apostolic as well, as they pushed King Josiah, King of Judah into purpose. He was now able to strategically bring about a national reform. Not only for the city of Jerusalem but nationally, touching the Kingdom of Judah. This reform consisted of the following:

KING JOSIAH'S

APOSTOLIC IMPLEMENTATIONS

1) Brought out vessels made for Baal and for the grove and burned them outside the city of Jerusalem.

2) Put down idolatrous priests who had authority to minister in the region.

3) Broke down the houses of the sodomites that stood in close proximity to the house of the Lord.

4) Destroyed high places of idolatry.

5) Destroyed fire worship to molech.

6) Removed sun worship.

7) Destroyed idolatrous altars.

8) Destroyed Jeroboam's altar.

9) Destroyed high places in Samaria.

10) Destroyed all traffic with demons and household gods.

11) Killed idolatrous priests.

12) Restored the Passover.

Josiah's response to the word was appropriate. The breaking to pieces of idolatrous items and the destruction of idolatrous principles was right and good. Though God's wrath was not lessened, the power of intervention directly into the region of Josiah in Jerusalem yielded change seen in the results demonstrated by Josiah, the ability to break through, tear down, and bring reform, was prevalent. Apostolic intervention had once again interrupted or upset the status quo.

CHAPTER X

APOSTOLIC EMANCIPATORS

Two American women's names have been recognized for their bravery and strength to bring forth a nation of people who had been considered as inhuman, to a place of dignity and freedom. These women are Sojourner Truth and Harriet Ross-Tubman.

SOJOURNER TRUTH

(1797 – 1883)

"During the reign of Ramses II (Pharaoh of Egypt) in the 19th dynasty about 1270 BC ," [24] under this rulership the Israelites experienced a life of slavery, which is a life of humiliation and intimidation, a people chosen by God. Through a plan of God, the Israelites were delivered from the house of bondage through His (God) servant Moses, who had grown up in Ramses I, through a plan of God (see Chapter VI) (Apostolic Intervention). Moses can be considered an Apostolic emancipator, however, this chapter will focus on and challenge women who experienced humiliation and intimidation in America during the 18th and 19th centuries. They experienced inhumanness at the hands of brutal slave masters in a land that was considered free. Since this was not the case, God again brought forth and designated strong and daring women to initiate and implement an Exodus II and to change the mindsets of persons who had been bound in slavery to realize that they are human and should embrace self worth.

Isabella (Sojourner Truth's birth name) was born in the late 1790's (records of the birth and death of slaves were not recorded). Most slaves could not read or write. Occasionally, the master's wives or children would in secrecy teach the "house slaves," those who worked in the master's house, to read or write.

If a slave was caught reading or writing outside of this setting, they were beaten, sometimes, to death. The reason for such extreme measures was to keep the slaves ignorant, for where there was ignorance there was fear and poverty. Jane C. McFann confirms these measures in a periodical Reading Today. It reads, according to Janet Duitsman Cornelius in, When I Can Read My Title Clear: Literacy, Slavery, and Religion in the Antebellum South (University of South Carolina Press, 1991):

> *"For enslaved African-Americans, literacy was more than a path to individual freedom. It was a communal act, a political demonstration of resistance to oppression and of self-determination for the Black community."* [25]

The U.S. had a law enforced in the southern states during and after slavery, known as "The Law of Ignorance." It remained there until the late 1970's. The spirit of that law, yet affects many African-Americans, causing them to often avoid reading or view it as a task. However, during the tormenting years of slavery, Jane C. McFann declares:

> *"Many slaves in the United States viewed learning to read as a way to free themselves from intellectual imprisonment. This fear can be seen in laws that were passed in many southern states. According to research done by Cornelius,*

legislation passed in Georgia in 1829 mandated 'fines, whipping, or imprisonment for anyone teaching slaves or free Blacks to read or write.'" [26]

Isabella's birthplace was Rosendale, New York in Ulster County. Yes, slavery was also common and practiced in New York, Maryland, and other states that we do not often consider as "slavery territory." However, slavery in the south was often more vicious than in the north.

She was born under the rulership of Colonel Johannis Hardenbergh, a Dutch immigrant. Her parents were James and Elizabeth, known as Betsey. Though she had about ten or eleven sisters and brothers, she was unable to bond with them due to laws of selling slaves to other plantation owners. This procedure separated families treacherously. Wives and husbands were sold separately and children were sold from their parents and separated from each other often in the process. This kind of inhuman treatment fosters outrageous fears, bitterness, and hatred for slave masters. It introduced a fragmented family design for the African-American and induced a silent non-trust agreement among slaves, including family members and a false trust in the hope of gaining freedom.

Note the following example:

Hardenbergh's son and heir, Charles, removed James and Betsey from their cottage to his great stone house. Here Isabella and the other slaves slept in a cold, dark, and damp cellar that bred illnesses of the joints and lungs. It was in the dark of this miserable pit that her parents told little Isabella the horror of the kidnapping of two of her siblings, Nancy (three) and Michael (five), some years before. A story more often retold, its anguish-ing details were still vivid in Sojourner Truth's memory nearly half a century later. [27]

Isabella was herself sold for $100.00 after the death of her master, Charles Hardenbergh. Her parents had grown old at this point, and unable to work, considered useless for plantation owners, and left to live in a hut to die of starvation, cold weather, sickness, disease, and poverty.

Isabella later had many visions, which she claimed were visions of Jesus Christ. She found solace in experiencing the love and presence of Jesus. She even likened one of her experiences to that of Paul's "Damascus Road" experience. From this point on she secured and maintained a job which brought her liberty until her son Peter was sold around 1826. This experience tested her faith. She believed that God would help her to recover him, which recovery was practically unheard of during slavery. But through a series of events in about a year she recovered him, only to be disappointed that he hardly knew her or responded to her. This was surely the result of the brutality that the child personally experienced and witnessed. The following account explains:

"The processing of getting Peter back took about a year, but by the spring of 1828, while Isabella was working at the Rutzers', Peter returned to Kingston. It was a homecoming that nearly broke his mother's heart. When his master brought Peter to Isabella, the child shrieked piteously and refused to go to her. Regarding his mother as though she were a monster, he clung to his 'dear master,' with whom he begged to stay. Isabella was utterly disconcerted. She knew she had gotten out of her place and run afoul of a prominent

family by going to court, and here, at the culmination of her efforts, her boy was hysterically denying her. She could lose her child and her year's efforts through his refusal to acknowledge her as his mother. Isabella had no way of knowing that Peter's response after so tragic a separation was characteristic of children who feel themselves abandoned by the adult to whom they are most attached, no matter what the objective circumstances of the loss.

Peter had over the course of this most traumatic year become detached from Isabella, the second stage of his reaction to the loss of his mother. At first, when he had been sold away, he would have been deeply distressed, disconsolate, and despairing. Isabella was seeing the middle stage, when, reunited with his mother, he acted as though she were a terrible stranger. In the third stage, after reconciling with her, he would have become intensely clinging and perhaps aggressive and defiant. This kind of behavior might help explain why Isabella took Peter with her to New York City instead of leaving him in Ulster County with his father and his sisters." [28]

Having experienced visions of Jesus as well as the baptism of the Holy Spirit, Isabella prepared herself for battle. This included changing her name from Isabella to Sojourner truth. Initially, she chose a first name Sojourner, but desired to have a last name. Therefore, she chose Truth because it typified what she believed was her mission to defy the cruelty of slavery and unacceptable treatment for women. Nell Irvin Painter so aptly describes the reasoning behind Isabella's name change as she states:

"Isabella had a long-standing pre-occupation with truth. As a girl she had been beaten and sexually abused, as an enslaved worker her word had been subject to disbelief and as a litigant reclaiming her honesty, she was liable to be doubted in situations of the utmost seriousness." [29]

As a sojourner, Sojourner Truth traveled as an itinerant preacher and a self-styled prophet. In 1843, she spent the summer walking through Long Island and Connecticut. Sleeping wherever shelter was available. Her work for food consisted of singing and teaching at camp meetings or churches. Often she preached in the streets.

Her life was devoted to lecturing and preaching against slavery and fighting for women's rights. Though her speech was not elegant, she captivated her audience with her six-foot frame, her guttural Dutch accent (original slave master was Dutch) and her faith in God.

Often mistaken as a man, she stood firm for rights for women. She spoke out against their inability to vote. The city of Akron, Ohio was impacted by the intervention of this emancipator.

In 1851 doubting her right to speak—announcing her intervention would be brief—Truth asked for and was granted permission to speak in one of the most interesting speeches of the Ohio Woman's Rights Convention. According to a report by Marius Robinson, a reporter for *The Bugle,* Truth addressed three aspects of women's identity: work, mind, and biblical precept. She demands rights for women by virtue of her own physical equality with men.

"Her examples come from her time in rural slavery, and her work is the work of the farm, which even in the industrializing 1850's, Americans, saw as the symbol of their economy." [30]

Her acceptance to speak at this convention gained her national respect. Her speech was included in the local newspapers. Akron's citizens were more enlightened than ever before by the presence and speech delivered by Sojourner Truth.

She continued to travel and carry, even sell, her narrative, that later became very famous.

In 1862, Abraham Lincoln signed the District of Columbia Emancipation Act, and the Emancipation Proclamation in 1863. Later, in 1864, she was honored to meet President Lincoln, a characteristic of Apostles and prophets to receive audience with heads of state.

"Her work was not confined to anti-slavery and women's rights alone, but embraced all human rights that were being encroached upon or denied." [31]

Sojourner Truth was an Apostolic emancipator blazing the trails to freedom.

HARRIET ROSS-TUBMAN

(1820 – 1913)

The birth of Harriet Ross (later married John Tubman) brought intervention to the Eastern Shores of Maryland, that would someday serve as a safety route to freedom.

"Strong as a man, brave as a lion, cunning as a fox," Harriet Tubman undoubtedly ran one of the greatest underground railroads of her time. The Underground Railroad was a network of individuals assisting slaves on their route to freedom. Some historians claim that she was the founder of the underground railroad.

Several years later after marrying John Tubman, a free man—(though this fact did not automatically yield her freedom)—her slave master died, and she heard rumors that his slaves would be sold out of the state. Harriet was determined, through divine guidance from God that she could and would escape to safety.

According to Marcy Heidish's research:

"She was deeply religious and often spoke of Divine warning, which she felt quickened her. She also experienced visionary states. She told Sarah Bradford, author, that she spoke with the Lord everyday as she would with a friend. According to Bradford, she felt prompted by mystical voices to escape bondage and had presentiment of danger to her father before she rescued him, and a graphic precognitive dream about John Brown, an anti-slavery activist." [32]

Previously, as a young girl, about thirteen years old, she received a blow to her head with a two-pound weight by a slave master that fractured her skull. She later recovered to a great extent, but suffered for years with fainting and sleeping spells. This however, did not deter her in the later years from escaping. Her first trip was indeed successful, as she returned many times to the Eastern Shores of Maryland to rescue family members first, then any slaves who were alert when she arrived on the plantations, late in the night, and were prepared to travel. When they heard her code spirituals and whistles, they arose.

The power of the sounds which are birthed in various seasons to communicate a message through songs, are often captured by Apostles who understand the times and seasons and are able to translate that sound into a new song through worship warfare. One of the songs used to communicate the "getaway" from the plantation was "Steal Away." Contrary to the understanding of many ministers of the gospel, "Steal Away" is not a defeated song or a "scapegoat to go to heaven." It is a code, which signaled to the slaves that Moses was on the plantation and deliverance was imminent.

Note the words:

> ***Steal away, steal away***
> ***Steal away to Jesus***
> ***Steal away***
> ***Steal away home***
> ***I ain't got long to stay here*** [33]

"Steal Away" meant it is time to gather belongings and travel. "I ain't got long" indicated a need to hurry.

Often referred to as a General, she eventually was thought of and referred to as "Moses."

She acknowledged as well, that God had called her to deliver her people out of bondage. Harriet is considered to have made over nineteen trips on the Underground Railroad and delivered over three hundred passengers to freedom. It is very possible and more feasible that the years traveling back and forth from Maryland to Philadelphia, Pennsylvania, the Liberty City, and sometimes Canada, that she may have made over three-hundred trips and delivered approximately three-thousand slaves from bondage to freedom. Nevertheless, she never experienced fatalities among any of her fugitives, nor was anyone recaptured.

A $40,000 reward was posted for Tubman's capture. It was considered dangerous to help slaves (personal property of slave owners) to escape, but Harriet Tubman continued to set the captives free. She had a mandate and was determined to fulfill it, even her return to the most dangerous Thompson plantation, in Maryland after many years, to rescue her mother and father.

Often referred to as a "General," she served in the Union Army during the civil war as scout, spy, and nurse. She is said to have foreseen the civil war in a vision, and desired to serve as a volunteer. She received an endorsement from Governor John A. Andrew of Massachusetts and traveled to Beaufort, South Carolina, where she was seized by Federal forces. Tubman reported to "Major General David Hunter, commander of the Department of the South, who gave her a pass to travel on the government transports." [34]

A significant event of note took place during Mrs. Tubman's service in the Union Army, which continues to demonstrate her Apostolic mandate to liberate the captives. "In 1863, she led the Union Army on a raid which resulted in the freedom of over 750 slaves." [35]

When the war was over, Harriet Tubman founded the Harriet Tubman Home for Indigent Aged Negroes. She also was instrumental in supporting and building the African Methodist Episcopal Church in Auburn, New York. She was the first woman to be ordained by the AME

Church as well. In 1896, she came into possession of a 25-acre farm and deeded it to the AME Church.

Tubman retired in her home, debt-free in 1869. Ms. Tubman married again in the same year, having been widowed two years prior. She married Nelson Davis, a civil war veteran.

Harriet Tubman died on March 10, 1913 and was buried with military honors in Auburn's Fort Hill Cemetery. Her impact is yet recognized in the City of Auburn.

The honors that she received in death were greater than those in her own country in life; yet her reward was great, for this great woman of God led many souls from bondage to freedom. She received the following revelation from the voice of God about her life:

"Suffering produces endurance. Endurance produces character. Character produces faith; and faith in the end will not disappoint."

CHAPTER XI

MARKETPLACE
TRAILBLAZERS – CUTTING
THE EDGE OF SLAVERY

As the Emancipation Proclamation was released, there existed women who had a passion for launching their own businesses and establishing grade schools and colleges. In a time when the African American was forbidden to read, there were those persons, who insisted on making it happen. In a time when the so called Negro was challenged not to buy and sell in the marketplace, establishing their own businesses and owning land, there were those who were determined to make it happen.

The following women emerged as market place trailblazers, defying the stigma of slavery, launched businesses and established schools. They were Madam C. J. Walker and Mary McLeod Bethune.

MADAM C. J. WALKER

DECEMBER 23, 1867 – MAY 25, 1919

DELTA, LOUISIANA USA

Born five years after the Emancipation Proclamation, Madam C. J. Walker, then known as Sarah Breedlove, emerged with a dream. Interestingly, circumstances surrounding her birth set the pace for her to become a trailblazer for American history and business courses for entrepreneurs.

Two circumstances noted about her:

> *"She was born in 1867 on the plantation where General Ulysses S. Grant staged the 1863 Siege of Vicksburg and one of her brothers joined former slaves in the 1879 mass exodus to the North from Louisiana and Mississippi."* [36]

By the age of six, Sarah had become an orphan. She married at age fourteen and bore a daughter, A'Lelia. Her husband died about eight years later.

ST. LOUIS, MISSOURI

At an early and crucial point in her life she learned to be independent and industrious. She moved to St. Louis, Missouri and supported herself by washing clothing (a popular job for ex-slaves or post-slave women). This type of job would yield $1.50 a day. Education was now an option. She went to school at night.

Washerwomen like Sarah became the primary breadwinners for their families at the turn of the century. European immigrants crowded out the black American men. The jobs that would yield acceptable salaries to support a family were off-limits to the black man. So the women washed, making up over sixty percent of the work population's washerwomen.

Though finances were a struggle, Sarah remarried. Her concern now was to find out how to bring herself and her daughter out of an unacceptable living environment, rowdy crowds, and drunkenness. She desired luxury and a secure environment. The dream was activated.

St. Louis, Missouri brought positive challenges beyond survival. Sarah began to desire self-improvement. Having met Charles Joseph Walker in the fall of 1902, she believed that he would be the proper companion for her.

Sarah Breedlove became involved with a community church, St. Paul AME Church.

> *"By Sunday, her only day off, Sarah welcomed the release that church services always brought her, for she had long embraced the power of prayer. As a newcomer to a fast city and a recent widow, she needed the solace it brought. Although she had attended the Pollard Church in Delta, she would later say that she had been 'converted' at St. Paul AME, the church one block away from her brothers' barbershop and six blocks from her first St. Louis home. That conversion to a deeper religious faith may have taken several months, or it may have occurred shortly after she arrived."* [37]

The church's elite membership of doctors, lawyers, teachers, and local dignitaries embracing a strong historical background caused Sarah to examine her appearance and mannerisms. She became more and more concerned about her hair texture and breakage. Texture in the early 20th century was a subtle issue in America. Kinky, curly hair has been equated with not attractive hair among African American women. Many women struggled with this.

Sarah later said, "I tried everything mentioned to me without any results." A'Lelia Bundles notes: "…her hair had begun breaking off and falling out. Her experimentation soon would lead to a solution, not just for her hair but for her life."

"THE DREAM"

> *" 'I was on the verge of becoming entirely bald,' Sarah often told other women. Ashamed of the 'frightful' appearance of her hair and desperate for a solution, she 'prayed to the Lord' for guidance. 'He answered my prayer,' she vouched. 'For one night I had a dream, and in that dream a big black man appeared to me and told me what to mix for my hair. Some of the remedy was from Africa, but I sent for it, mixed it, put it on my scalp and in a few weeks my hair was coming in faster than it had ever fallen out.' After obtaining the same results on her daughter and her neighbors, she later told a reporter, 'I made up my mind I would begin to sell it.' "* [38]

Following the dream, she began to experiment with what she had received in the dream and invested a day's earnings of $1.50 to begin her business, which quickly began to escalate.

DENVER, COLORADO

In 1906, Sarah Breedlove moved to Denver, Colorado. She had become successful with the business she established; the hair formula she believed was a miracle. It was in Colorado that she attained the now famous name, Madam C. J. Walker, after Sarah Breedlove married Charles J. Walker. Her discovery resulted in a hairdressing formula, which revolutionized the hair care industry and changed the looks of black women.

Introducing a method which would manage the hair of African-American women, including shampoos and pomade (an oil for hair growth), a hot straightening comb, which made the hair absolutely beautiful, she expanded her business to Pittsburgh, Pennsylvania and later Indianapolis, Indiana.

Many historical accounts regarding Madam Walker's inventions indicate that she invented the "straightening comb," an iron comb, when heated and pulled through curly or kinky hair resulted in longer length and lustrously manageable hair. On the other hand, A'Lelia clarifies the account as she precisely says:

> *"Equally persistent was the widely circulated and incorrect belief that Madam Walker had invented the straightening comb. In fact, this metal hair care implement probably had been sold when Parisian Marcel Grateau created his famous Marcel wave, and was advertised in Bloomingdale's and Sears catalogues during the 1880's and 1890's, presumably for the thousands of white women who also had kinky hair. Years later I would learn that the claim probably originated in 1922—three years after Madam Walker's death—when the Walker Company purchased the rights to a patent from the widow of a man who had manufactured combs for Madam Walker."* [39]

The Indiana plan serviced both the Pennsylvania and Indiana businesses.

"By 1919, the Madam C. J. Walker Manufacturing Company stretched an entire city block and provided employment for over three thousand people."

Madam Walker's accomplishments were outstanding. As a trailblazer, she came to be known as the first black female millionaire of modern times.

Missions also became a part of her desire and ambitions as she housed representatives from the AME church visiting from Africa.

These visitations inspired her to eventually establish scholarships for students at Tuskegee Institute in Tuskegee, Alabama. She desired to build a Tuskegee Institute in Africa from inspiration she received at St. Paul AME church in St. Louis, Missouri, where she first heard about foreign life from Bishops and Missionaries. She eventually bequeathed $100,000.00 toward construction of an academy for girls in West Africa. In addition, Madam Walker supported the efforts of educator, Mary McLeod Bethune, founder of Bethune-Cookman College, in Daytona, Florida. Additional philanthropies included sizable contributions to the NAACP.

A trailblazer for the market place, introducing and creating new innovations for the beauty field and building the self-esteem for the African-American woman, Madam C. J. Walker is to be commended. May the trail continue to open for others to travel as new Apostolic trailblazers emerge. The edge of slavery is no longer a hindrance. Entrepreneurs can move forward.

Mary Jane McLeod Bethune

1875 – 1955

The number seventeen has often been equated with that of victory. This seems to have been the case for Mary Jane McLeod Bethune, born the 17th child of slave parents Sam and Patsy McLeod in 1875, yet, the only child born free. Slavery held no claim to her birth nor enslavement to her mind.

Though she worked in the cotton-fields of South Carolina, she was able to attend school, excelling rapidly. So much so that she was noticed by a Quaker lady who paid for her to attend a boarding school.

When an individual has an Apostolic mandate, hindrances or obstacles become passage-ways for them to fulfill their mandate. Mary McLeod Bethune was one such person, who had an assignment to educate the Americans who were of African decent.

In the 20 – 21st Centuries, the need may appear to have been remote. Schools were in existence all over the United States, public and private. Small rural towns to large cities provided a place for African-Americans to study, as well as any one, regardless of national or ethnic background. On the other hand, prior to the late 20th century, this was not a fact in the United States, including Mayesville, South Carolina. After the age of 11, a school opened about five miles from Mary McLeod's home. This was a great blessing for her, even though she had to walk the distance. After graduation, a young Quaker woman in Denver, Colorado, who wanted to help one Black child attain more education, awarded her a small scholarship. Mary was selected and went on to attend Scotia Seminary in Concord, North Carolina, where she graduated in 1893. [40]

Miss McLeod desired so much to become a missionary to Africa, a terminology often used in the local church (African American), for women who experienced a call to live and work in foreign countries. If they were sent to the foreign fields, they often lived among the nationals for months, years, and for some, a lifetime, building schools and hospitals. The work is Apostolic in nature, but is mostly categorized as missions, persons fulfilling their call to ministry as missionaries.

Mary's case was greatly disappointing, after studying at Moody Bible Institute in Chicago, Illinois, she was denied a position to serve in Africa by the Presbyterian Board of Missions.

Later, Miss McLeod married Albertus Bethune and taught in several schools. She then began to take an obstacle and develop a passageway. Moving to Florida, she invested $1.50 to establish a school for girls in Daytona Beach, Florida. This city was destined to be impacted by the entrance and Apostolic presence of one of the greatest women of the 20th Century.

Her first school consisted of five students, located close to a city in an old house. Students paid 50 cents a week for tuition. She was able to obtain funding from Proctor and Gamble, as well as from John D. Rockerfeller. [41]

The school grew from a girl's boarding school to eventually a college, which after merging with Cookman Institute in 1929, became known as Bethune-Cookman College having a student body of 600 students, 32 faculty members as well as an $800,000 debt free campus.

As a marketplace trailblazer, she was highly recognized by governmental officials as follows:

1930 President Herbert Hoover appointed her to the White House Conference on Child Health.

1935 President Franklin D. Roosevelt appointed her director of the Office of Minority Affairs and the National Youth Administration.

1945 President Harry S. Truman appointed Bethune to the first conference of the United Nations.

The National Youth Administration (NYA) afforded an opportunity for Mrs. Bethune to travel extensively, to interact with many nations and establish schools for minorities, which provided them a quality education.

In addition to the outstanding government posts that Mrs. Bethune held, this marketplace trailblazer was responsible for founding the following organizations:

> The National Association of Colored Women
> The National Council of Negro Women
> Co-Founder—The Central Life Insurance Company
> (provided insurance to African Americans)

In 1952, Mrs. Bethune was the only female president of a national insurance company in the United States.

Mary McLeod Bethune has left an indelible mark on the national approach to education for minorities in America and the impact of the educational foundation that was blazed in Daytona Beach, Florida, will remain a vital part of the history and destiny of that city.

20th – 21st CENTURY APOSTLES IMPACTING THE CITIES

RESPONSES TO SURVEY

Bishop Bill Hamon
Christian International
Ministries Network
Santa Rosa Beach, Florida

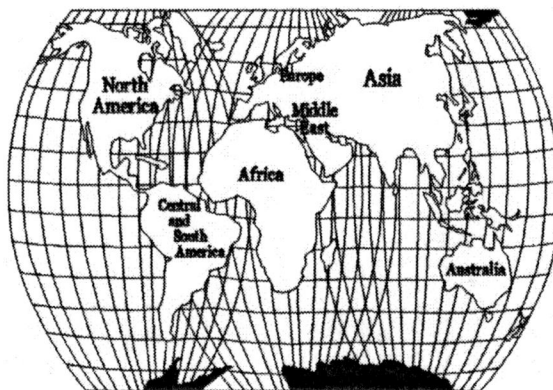

1. As a 21st Century Apostle, how would you describe your role?

"As Apostolic oversight of a network of ministers. I have an Apostolic revelation anointing of Ephesians 3:6 for bringing a revelation to the Body of Christ concerning God's times and purpose for restoration to the church. I have a foundation laying ministry of present Truth."

2. Have you encountered questions or concerns regarding the authenticity of the present day Apostles?

"I have been asked many questions and have done much Biblical research on Apostles. I have attended a round table of Apostles in several parts of the world. Apostles have authority in the sphere of their ministry but not everywhere or over everyone. Apostles have the gifted ability of Christ to govern and set things in order and work miracles."

3. Can you say you received a direct calling to this office?

"Yes. I have received many prophetic words through many prophets and Apostles from around the world."

4. Which city or cities do you believe your Apostolic presence and authority has impacted. Describe the impact and give time frames if possible.

"My anointing as Prophet has impacted many nations; mainly my own ministers, their churches, and local headquarters area. My Apostolic ministry has affected the corporate Body of Christ more by ministries mentioned under question #1."

5. How do you see the Apostolic role being shaped to meet the challenge of the 21st Century?

"Apostles must release Apostolic wisdom for their part in building the Church. Apostles need to teach, train, activate and mature saints in the church into the vocal and revelation gifts of the Holy Spirit. We still do not know all the specialties of Apostles, etc."

Reverend Dr. Roderick Tay
Tentmakers International
Singapore

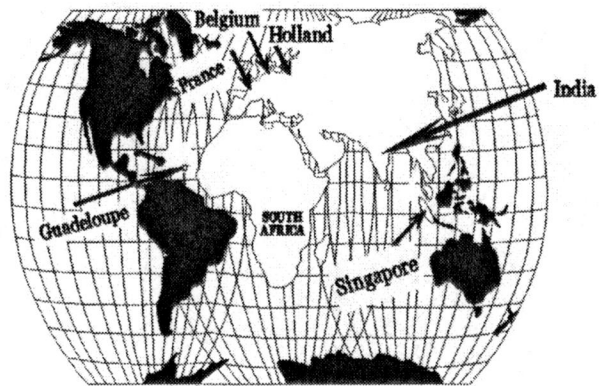

1. As a 21st Century Apostle how would you describe your role?

"My role is overseeing pastors and their ministries. Also training and mentoring businessmen. Pioneering and pastoring a new local ministry. Consulting with and counseling numerous leadership and entrepreneurs."

2. Have you encountered questions or concerns regarding the authenticity of the present day Apostles?

"Sometimes, a brief explanation of the Apostolic age and more of the Holy Spirit would suffice."

3. Can you say you received a direct calling to this office?

"Yes. God called me to plant over 1,000 churches on the planet of the earth. In my last ministry, the figure has reached 557 churches. Praise the Lord. In the present day ministry—there have been 30 more churches being planted."

4. Which city or cities do you believe your Apostolic presence and authority has impacted? Describe the impact and give time frames if possible.

"Guadeloupe; Belgium; Dordreche, Holland; Paris, France; Manila, Philippines; Hyderabad, India; Johannesburg, South Africa."

5. How do you see the Apostolic role being shaped to meet the challenges of the 21st Century?

"I believe God is creating and developing new ideology and dimension of the application of the Apostolic and prophetic anointing. For instance, in Seoul, Korea—the Cell Group movement; in Singapore, a youth movement that produced 13,000 strong church members. Another ministry in Singapore has a strong emphasis on biblical economics has produced a congregation of 8000 church members. Amen!"

97

Apostle Ernest Leonard, Senior Pastor
Provision of Promise Ministries
Newark, New Jersey

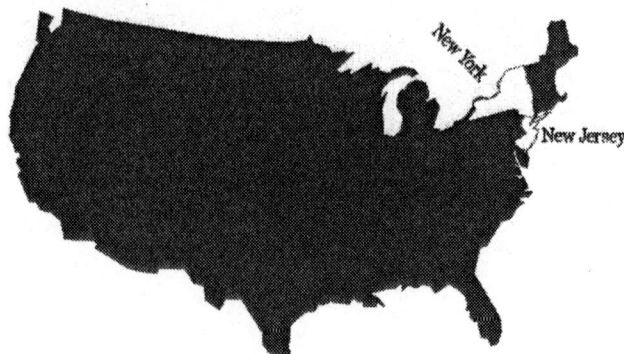

1. As a 21st Century Apostle, how would you describe your role?

"My role is that of an Apostle, an individual called to raise up 5-fold ministry gift leaders through Apostolic impartation that they too may understand and impact according to their gift/office into others."

2. Have you encountered questions or concerns regarding the authenticity of the present day Apostles?

"Yes, Usually those questions do not challenge the authenticity as opposed to understanding the difference in the present day reformation and the religious denomination.

3. Can you say you received a direct calling to this office?
   "Yes."

4. Which city or cities do you believe your Apostolic presence and authority has impacted. Describe the impact and give time frames if possible.

"New Jersey and New York Regions – Besides the establishment of a school of the Apostles, whereby individuals learn of the Apostolic Reformation Movements. I've also coordinated deliverance seminars weekly in New York, teaching and demonstrating the necessity of deliverance in this present move of God."

5. How do you see the Apostolic role being shaped to meet the challenges of the 21st Century?

"The movements of God will be multi-faceted and the challenge is for us as Apostolic believers to keep up with the various movements of God, quickly to execute and promote changes that are necessary to receive fresh impartations and revelation for each season of change."

Apostle Idell Cheever
Headquarters/International
Savannah, Georgia

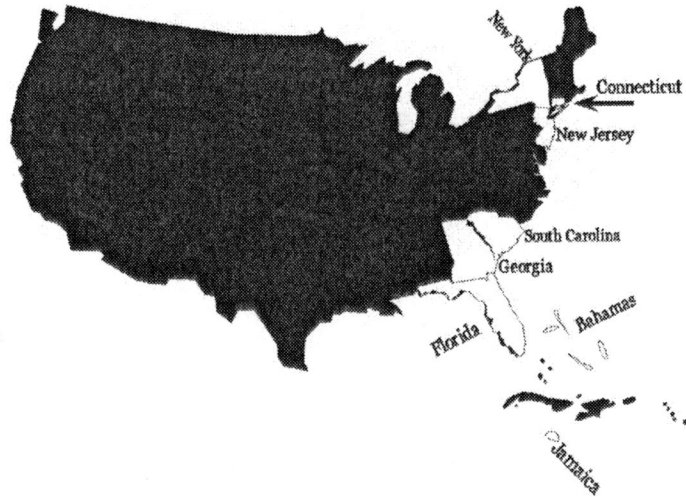

1. As a 21st Century Apostle how would you describe your role?

"I would describe my role as a 21st Century Apostle as follows: It is described in the life of the Apostle Paul, as a partner/servant leader with Jesus Christ, not only founding and establishing ministries, wherever the spirit directs, but making and building leaders to go forth taking the kingdom of God."

2. Have you encountered questions or concerns regarding the authenticity of the present day Apostles?

"Yes, I have encountered questions regarding the authenticity of the present day Apostle. (a) Many say there are no Apostles in our day and if there be any, they definitely cannot be a woman. But in this I have no fight simply because, I know who I am, and who called and anointed me to be an Apostle."

3. Can you say you received a direct calling to this office?

"I can say I did receive a direct call to this office in the month of September 1986, when I was anointed, or should I say consecrated to this office. Although I had been walking in the office of Apostle/prophet most of my saved life."

4. Which city or cities do you believe your Apostolic presence and authority has impacted. Describe the Impact and give time frames if possible.

"A few of the cities and states where my Apostolic presence and authority has impacted are Georgia, (Savannah, Macon, Augusta, Waycross, Newington, Baxley, Jesup, Guyton, Brunswick, Darin, St. Marys, Claxton); Florida (Jacksonville, Palatka, Ocala, Orlando, Miami, Ft. Lauderdale, Glenncove); South Carolina, (Burton, Hardeeville, Beaufort, Buck Island, Estill, Ridgeland; Connecticut, (Stamford); New Jersey, (Newark); New York City, West Indies, Germany, Bahamas Islands, Spanish Town Jamaica and Independence City,

99

Jamaica. And the impact was the establishing of ministries."

5. How do you see the Apostolic role being shaped to meet the challenges of the 21st Century?

"The Apostolic ministry is finally coming back into it's rightful place in the body of Christ, for centuries the Apostolic ministry has been placed in the background in the world of Christendom, but in this 21st Century the order of God is back in focus and shall be the ministry that shall bring the body of Christ back into unity and produce the fullness of Christ in the earth, preparing men and women to rule and reign with Christ right here on this earth."

Apostle Jonas Clark
Spirit of Life Ministries
Hallandale Beach, Florida

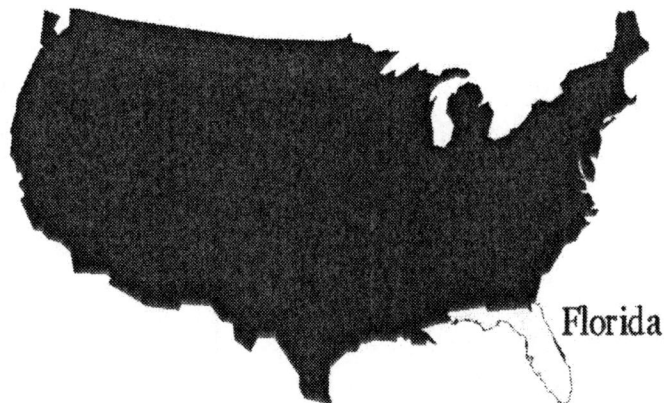

Florida

1. As a 21st Century Apostle how would you describe your role?

"My role is to bring about an Apostolic identity and purpose to the body of Christ. When the church recognizes the distinct and separate differences between all five-fold ascension gifts of Apostles, prophets, evangelist, pastors and teachers then she will be able to benefit from those differences."

2. Have you encountered questions or concerns regarding the authenticity of the present day Apostles?

"Challenging the biblical role of Apostles and modern Apostolic ascension gifts is not valid once we understand the differences between Apostles and pastors. There are modern day Apostles just like there are modern day prophets. Jesus taught us to judge according to the fruit of one's ministry not according to titles. An Apostle told me recently that he was asked, 'By what authority do you call yourself an Apostle?' His response was, 'By what authority do you call yourself a pastor.' "

3. Can you say you received a direct calling to this office?

"The calling of an Apostle is like every other ascension gift—by Jesus Christ alone. Although one can be called to be an Apostle, it is more likely that there would be some sort of progressive training before one is ready to enter that role. Every ascension gift carries different responsibility. The Apostle Paul is a good example of one who raised up sons who were called into ministry. He had many spiritual sons who worked with him, including Timothy, Silas, and Titus. Paul teaches us that sonship under an Apostolic father prepares you for Apostleship later. The key is to be faithful where you are at the time."

4. Which city or cities do you believe your Apostolic presence and authority has impacted. Describe the impact and give time frames if possible.

"I think that it is too soon to examine the overall impact of the restoration of the Apostolic anointing. People are still coming into an understanding of roles and operations. Therefore, the influence and impact of an Apostle on a territory will only be seen after a life time of hard work."

5. How do you see the Apostolic role being shaped to meet the challenges of the 21st Century?

"The role of every ascension gift is to spiritually equip every believer to enter the work of the ministry. In South Florida we spell work—S-W-E-A-T. The Apostolic anointing specifically opens the eyes of every believer to the importance of the local church. From the 'gathering only' paradigm to the Apostolic 'sending' dimension; from the one-man-only mentality to teamwork, or their responsibility to the success of the local church as builders; to working as a team player with an assigned task, specific goals and targets. Being equipped and 'sent'—ones, rather than 'went'—ones, who are disciple makers. Becoming panoramic with a global vision rather than a local-church-only vision. The need of spiritual fathers who are called to transition the sons into maturity. What can we expect for the 21st Century? In one word—change. We can expect the Apostolic anointing to place a strong demand on the body of Christ to grow and complete the harvest of lost souls."

Apostle Buddy Crum
Life Center Ministries
Atlanta, Georgia 30338

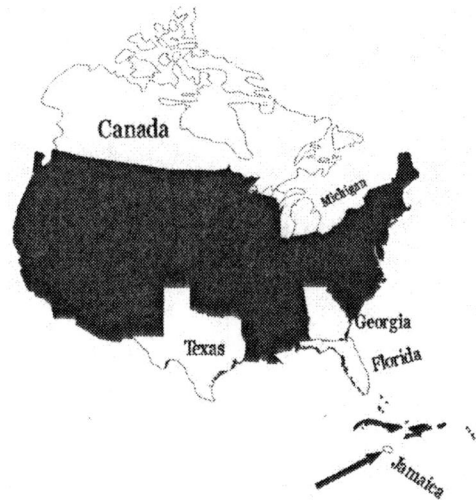

1. As a 21st Century Apostle how would you describe your role?

"Apostolic leadership of a local church—Apostolic leadership in marketplace ministries—to provide strategies and direction for Brokenness Ministry."

2. Have you encountered questions or concerns regarding the authenticity of the present day Apostles?

"Yes, in written communication."

3. Can you say you received a direct calling to this office?

"Yes, Bishop Hamon, as a prophet, released the calling."

4. Which city or cities do you believe your Apostolic presence and authority has impacted. Describe the impact and give time frames if possible.

"Working through Christian International at Santa Rosa, Florida, we have established many points of influence in Georgia, Florida, Texas, Canada, Atlanta, Detroit, Dallas, Kingston, Jamaica and Chapters of Christian International Business Network (C.I.B.N.)"

5. How do you see the Apostolic role being shaped to meet the challenges of the 21st Century?

"Paradigm shift; boldness, changing wineskins from one gift (pastor to five gifts)—changing focus from the local church to the Kingdom of God—strategies for reaching nations."

Apostle Ronald Harden
Christ Temple of Refuge
Milledgeville, Georgia

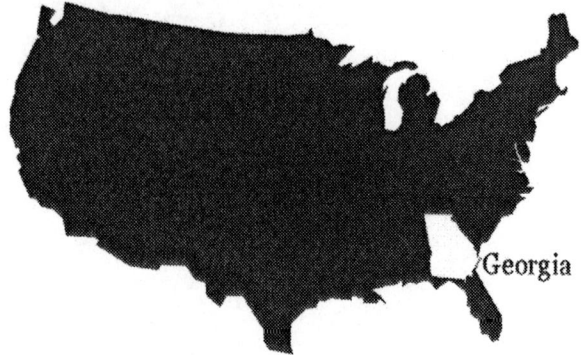

Georgia

1. As a 21st Century Apostle how would you describe your role?

My mandate can be summarized and enumerated as follows:

a. *To foster greater knowledge and understanding of the five-fold ministry, especially the restoration of the prophetic and Apostolic offices to the body of Christ.*

b. *To teach and train present day prophets and Apostles in the administration and execution of their respective offices; further to raise up a prophetic people sensitive to the move of the spirit.*

c. *To proclaim the long ago abandoned "Gospel of the Kingdom," to a greater extent, to demonstrate the Kingdom of God before men in all cultures. This fact recognizes that every kingdom must be brought under the Lordship of Christ.*

d. *To stand steadfastly against the prevailing evils of society, especially cults, the occult, and demonic strongholds.*

e. *To guard against the infiltration of false doctrines and the spirit of deception in the Body of Christ.*

f. *To fan the flames of revival that will usher in the Kingdom of God.*

g. *To urge recognition of other neglected doctrines of the church, namely the Restoration of the Tabernacle of David, Restoration of the Nine Gifts of the Holy Spirit, and the recognition of God's manifest presence in the church.*

2. Have you encountered questions or concerns regarding the authenticity of the present day Apostles?

"Skepticism regarding the authenticity of present day Apostles is pervasive in the world and in the church as well. I surmise that acceptance of this office will develop gradually, but only after the skeptics are hard pressed to deny its demonstration."

3. Can you say you received a direct calling to this office?

"I did, in fact, receive a direct call to this office. To my chagrin, I was also instructed to employ the title publicly whenever the opportunity presented itself."

4. Which city or cities do you believe your Apostolic presence and authority has impacted. Describe the impact and give time frames if possible.

"My greatest impact would be upon the Middle Georgia Area, particularly during the years of 1984 – present. To some degree, this ministry has been effective in all areas cited in the first question above. I would like to add, however, that the Middle Georgia Area was very resistant to the Apostolic/prophetic schemata of God. Being one of the forerunners in this calling, exacted a heavy toll I oft times try to forge. Now, of course, others who have been called to these offices are not without an existing paradigm to emulate."

5. How do you see the Apostolic role being shaped to meet the challenges of the 21st Century?

"If there is a challenge to the 21st Century Apostle at all, it is the challenge to be relevant to an ever changing, multi-faceted, diverse culture and people (s). Herein lies the failure of Christianity. The proliferation of Islam, liberation theology, and the like, can be attributed to our inability to make the gospel relevant to the lives of men. We preached heaven, but we forgot that the Kingdom of God is 'among us.'

There are perhaps two other areas worthy of mention:

a. During the recent attacks on the World Trade Towers, I asked (rather publicly) 'Where are God's prophets and Apostles?' Surely, our governmental leaders need a sure word from God in times of national and international crises!
b. With the emergence of psychics in such public roles as advisors to law enforcement, counselors and healers to the hurting, inquisitive, and 'magi' to presidents, surely I ask, would not the world turn from this if they knew something better existed—the real thing? Undoubtedly, we must come forward, and we must be relevant."

Apostle Dr. Pernell H. Hewing
The Sanctuary
Whitewater, Wisconsin

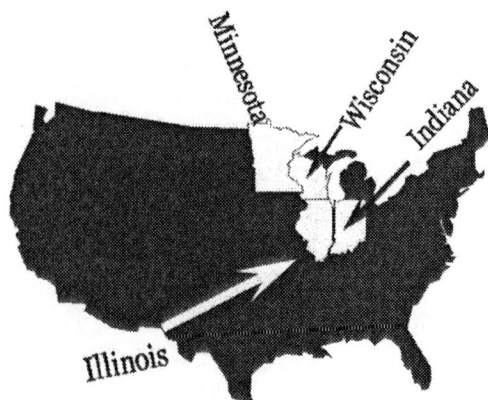

1. As a 21st Century Apostle how would you describe your role?

"One with the specific calling for the End-Time Church. I believe that I am called to prepare End-Time Saints for the End-Time Battle of the Age. Inextricably interwoven into my role is to prepare the Saints for the Saints Movement, which is the movement which we are now in or we are approaching rapidly. The Lord is releasing gifts and graces in the church upon the Saints, and the Saints must be prepared for this End-Time move of God.

My role also is to prepare the Five-Fold Ministers for leadership in the Apostolic/Prophetic Church. My main role under-girding my call is to prepare intercessors to open the way for this final move of the Church. This includes bringing forth true intercessors which include the Saints and the Five-fold ministers."

2. Have you encountered questions or concerns regarding the authenticity of the present day Apostles?

"I have not had questions asked me directly about the authenticity of the present-day Apostle, but I know many who come around me have that question. I have not dealt with the question because I don't stop what God has given me to do to deal with what others are saying about the authenticity of God's movements. That may sound arrogant, but I have been criticized so much as pioneer, so much of what I do is questioned until it is established and moving. Perhaps I should be prepared to deal with this question."

3. Can you say you received a direct calling to this office?

"Yes, I did receive a definite call from the Lord even when I had no idea that I had entered into the call and was doing the work of an Apostle long before God called me. After many years of laying foundations and establishing ministers and ministries, God spoke to me through Ephesians 1:1. He said to me,

106

'Who are You?' Paul knew who he was, who called him and for what purpose. Now, you tell me 'who are you?' After several weeks of pondering the question and working through the thoughts of the role of women in the ministry, the Lord let me know if I did not admit to the call of Apostle, He would not recognize me in what I was doing. I then admitted my call to God. A few months later, Dr. Jim Davis, an affiliate with Christian International, came to my Five-Fold Ministry Conference and before he left, He said, 'You are not a pastor, you are an Apostle. I am going back and tell Bishop Hamon and see if he will ordain you as an Apostle.' That was August, and in October of that same year, Bishop Hamon ordained me as an Apostle."

4. Which city or cities do you believe your Apostolic presence and authority has impacted. Describe the impact and give time frames if possible.

"The Lord specifically gave me four states with a present focus on three of them. They are Minnesota, Wisconsin, Illinois, and Indiana. He kept me working in Minnesota for several years establishing training—even a branch of my Theological School of ministry and several intercessory Prayer Training groups. He has now focused my work in Wisconsin, Illinois, and Indiana."

5. How do you see the Apostolic role being shaped to meet the challenges of the 21st Century?

"I see the Apostle's role as a must for this End-Time, New Testament Church of the 21st Century. It is being shaped slowly because all too many churches have not recognized what God is doing in the Church; therefore, they do not recognize the role of the Apostle. I believe it will be some time before the role of the Apostle is fully recognized by the established church. The Church is at the same transitional era it was when John the Baptist and Jesus Christ came on the scene, closed out the Law, and opened the way for the Holy Spirit and the Church age. All we can do is what God is doing, and the Lord will fulfill the call of the age."

Apostle Jim Erb
New Wilmington, Pennsylvania

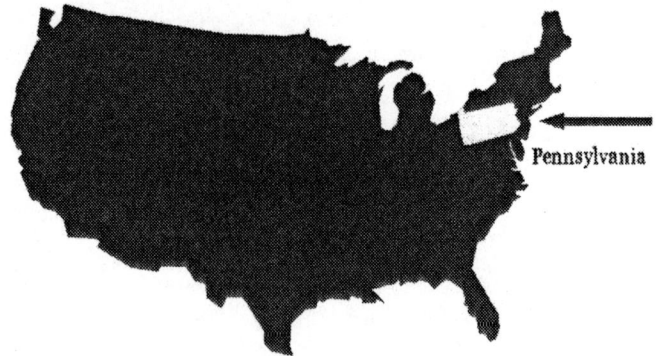

Pennsylvania

1. As a 21st Century Apostle how would you describe your role?

"Overseeing a network of ministers, churches and ministries. Pastoring leaders – helping them to know and fulfill their calling."

2. Have you encountered questions or concerns regarding the authenticity of the present day Apostles?

"Yes."

3. Can you say you received a direct calling to this office?

"Yes."

4. Which city or cities do you believe your Apostolic presence and authority has impacted. Describe the impact and give time frames if possible.

"Central Western Pennsylvania.—life long resident (67 years old)—Network has existed for approximately 5 years."

5. How do you see the Apostolic role being shaped to meet the challenges of the 21st Century?

"Equipping saints for the marketplace by 5-fold ministry equipping teams."

Apostle Dr. John Neuhaus
Zion Foundation Tabernacle
Lauderhill, Florida

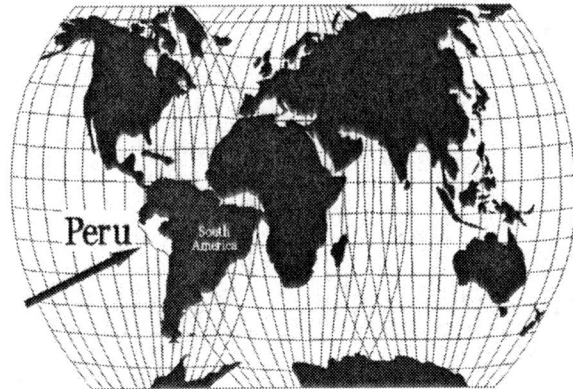

1. As a 21st Century Apostle how would you describe your role?

"Apostles like prophets are sent forth in the wisdom of God as special emis-saries from the very throne room of God (Luke 11:49). They carry with them a vital word of present truth to the body of Christ. The Apostle is commissioned as the Lord's chosen instruments of change, reform and restoration. In their divine commission they bring direction, encouragement and correction with the specific purpose of empowering and advancing the church in the earth. These Apostles will be like the Joshua and Judges of old who will, with author-ity, command a new generation to move forward, obtain and walk in the prom-ises of God. This will empower the church to move from a wandering wilderness experience to an organized and disciplined army that will operate as true warriors with power and authority in the Kingdom of love and judg-ment. The mobilized army will overcome great obstacles even penetrating the Jerichos and the walled cities of the earth to bring deliverance.

The Apostle's divine commission is to advance the church into a greater level of power, unity and teamwork. This mobilization will activate the armies of the living God to exercise their God given abilities and their gifts for works and service in the Kingdom.

The Apostle is a leader and commander commissioned of the Lord to lead the church forward into higher dimensions of the spirit. They further activate anointed strategies for the purpose of bringing in the harvest, take new terri-tory and advance the Kingdom of God in the earth."

2. Have you encountered questions or concerns regarding the authenticity of the present day Apostles?

"Yes. Opposition becomes almost natural to the Apostle because they confront outdated mindsets, religious spirits and bring change and reform to the church.

Jesus taught his disciples, which he named Apostles, that persecution and opposition would come and they were even to expect it. Every true Apostle will encounter opposition even as the first century Apostles did. This opposition comes directly from Satan and the principalities that Satan rules because his works are exposed and his territory is threatened.

Because the ministry of the Apostle is not easily defined or understood, other leaders and carnal believers are sometimes intimidated and often misrepresent the God sent ministry of the body, which is set first in order and importance in the church. God has sent forth and saved this ministry for the last time to restore order, pull down and overthrow everything, everyone and every mind-set that has exalted itself against the knowledge of God.

The Lord desires that all of his people have a clear view and a balanced perspective of his divine purpose in the earth. As Jesus made enemies and also some friends when he overturned the tables in the temple, so will the Apostles as they preach truth and set things in order.

Overturning things is not a pleasant ministry but a very needed one. Of those who are courageous enough and not intimidated by the false and impure motives of some in the Lord's house, the temple will again be cleaned. The lame and the blind will once again come into God's house to be healed because the Zeal of the Lord of Hosts will perform this."

3. Can you say you received a direct call from the Lord?

"In my case it was more of a promotion than a direct call. When the Lord called me it was to the office of the prophet. Then through the years the Lord trained me in the other aspects of ministry and the offices of evangelism, teaching and the pastorate for another ten years. As I proved faithful in this training I began to operate with the anointing of the Apostle and in deeper dimensions of the spirit with greater signs and wonders following my ministry. I found the word to be true 'he that is faithful in a little will be made ruler over much.' It has been my life and ministry experience that promotion truly does come from the Lord."

4. Which city or cities do you believe your Apostolic presence and authority has impacted. Describe the impact and give the time frames if possible.

"In my travels through thirteen countries the Lord has sent me to many remote cities and villages that few other ministries had reached or were willing to go because there were no offerings to bring home. We have imparted and taught the leaders of these cities and it has truly had a great impact on the people of those regions.

In the year 2000 the whole city of Piura, Peru came to the Lord. This conversion included the mayor and his wife. Since that time, God has even healed the land itself and crops are growing that would not grow before. People are returning to the region and the curse on the land has been broken.

Many miracles and healings have occurred in these cities. A meeting in Ambo, Peru saw over two hundred sick, blind, lame and infirmed people healed, including eleven deaf and dumb people. Three of those healed were totally deaf and dumb from birth. Other miracles and healings included tumors disappearing, teeth straightened, cancers healed and demons cast out."

5. How do you see the Apostolic role being shaped to meet the challenges of the 21st Century?

"The Apostles that come forth in this hour have already been shaped and prepared by the Lord himself in the last years of the 20th Century. They are prepared for the challenges of this new millennium and ready to lead the church into a new day. The Apostles are taking the church from the manna of the wilderness to eating and digesting a more mature word of the old corn of the land into the Kingdom age of glory, taking us from milk to meat. These Apostles have been prepared by the Lord beforehand just as the Apostle Paul had spent fourteen years being prepared by the Lord in the wilderness. We know that while in the wilderness God gave Paul the revelation of a new day and a new dispensation. This revelation allowed him to almost single-handedly move the church from being steeped in the law of Moses, to the liberty of the gospel of the grace of God that the Apostle said was committed unto him.

Many of these Apostles will arrive on the scene as Elijah did with the word of the Lord in their mouth and heaven's authority to bring what they speak to pass. These will be the straight shooters of a polished shaft that have been hidden in God's quiver but will, like the Benjamites, not miss their mark.

Isaiah 49:2 : 'And he hath made my mouth like a sharp sword; in the shadow of his hand hath he hid me, and made me a polished shaft, in his quiver hath he hid me:'

These Apostles have been hidden and obscured in the shade of God's hand which is his five-fold ministry.
Apostles of the 21st Century will be mountain men like Abraham, Moses, and Jesus. They will be the saviors and deliverers of Obadiah that stand on Mount Zion where kings and priests rule, that will judge the mountain of Esau's flesh."

Apostle Nancy West
Outflow Ministries
Apostolic Prophetic
Teaching and Training
Redan, Georgia

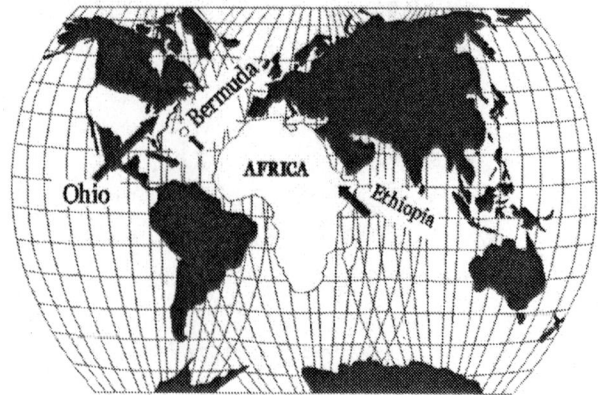

1. As a 21st Century Apostle how would you describe your role?

"I primarily function in the role of an Apostolic prophetic teacher, empowering others to know and fulfill their calling and destiny through revelatory teachings, prophetic insight and impartation. Also with wise counsel and relationship."

2. Have you encountered questions or concerns regarding the authenticity of the present day Apostles?

"Yes, as to the function of the present day Apostles compared to the Apostles in the book of Acts. No, to the authenticity of the present day Apostles who are not only functioning in the office but also in the demonstration of the power and authority of the office. Many have taken the title of Apostle but are not operating in the gifting of the office, nor the manifestation of the anointing that comes with the office."

3. Can you say you received a direct calling to this office?

"Yes, every since the day of my salvation experience, January 3, 1985, my heart has always been to serve the body of Christ. Specifically to come along side leaders and strengthen them in their ministry call and to leave a deposit in their local church for them to draw upon, under-girding their God given vision, for their community, city, state or nation. All the prophecies I have received in the last 5 years were that God had called me to be an Apostle and to pioneer the Apostolic woman."

4. Which city or cities do you believe your Apostolic presence and authority has impacted. Describe the Impact and give time frames if possible.

"I believe the Apostolic presence and authority in my life has impacted Mount Vernon, Ohio, where I spent three weeks teaching and raising up a trained prophetic intercession team. As we went into strategic focused spiritual warfare,

the atmosphere over the region changed. They met once a week heralding the vision of the church with the Sr. Pastor present and continuing in prophetic intercession until things started changing in the natural and in the spirit. They now only meet once a month but they are experiencing renewal, refreshing and revival within their midst. The dates that I was there were December 18, 2000 – January 8, 2001. Out of that time came the Apostolic Prophetic Intercession and spiritual warfare teachers, students, answer key manuals and a power point presentation.

Also, I believe my Apostolic presence and authority impacted Bermuda and Addis Abba, Ethiopia. At a conference in Bermuda in a denominational church, the presence, power and authority of the Apostolic was released and ushered in a greater anointing that not only broke up fallow ground that was anchoring the saints in shallowness, bitterness, and unforgiveness but also released them into the ministering of spiritual gifts and more of Jesus evidenced in their life, with repentance that brought them into unity and the corporate anointing. That took place in September 2001.

When I went to Addis Abba, Ethiopia in December 2001 the women in ministry from Ethiopia told me that they do not receive women in ministry. I preached, taught and did some training of the prophetic, deliverance and intercession teams. It was an awesome time of mixing and blending gifts and anointing, which took each of the teams, church leaders and the saints of God to another level and realm of anointing that could be reproduced in others. The reproducing and impartation anointing on my life was released to them and we flowed together and each one of our lives was enhanced and built up to bring about a divine connection that was God ordained. I will be going back to Addis Abba, Ethiopia to found and establish the Christian International School of Ministry—this year. The school is to open in January 2003."

5. How do you see the Apostolic role being shaped to meet the challenges of the 21st Century?

"In the 21st Century the Apostolic movement that is producing the emergence of Apostles on the scene, demonstrating the power and authority of the office, collaborating together in the up building of the Kingdom with the prophets, heralding the word of the Lord, a merging of both offices aligned for the purpose of equipping and preparing the saints to operate in their gifts and calling; that will affect not only the church but the marketplace and government, reforming the way we 'know and do church'. All of the five-fold giftings: Pastor, Teacher, Evangelist, Apostle and Prophet working together in unity and the saints of God functioning in their God given talent, gifts and abilities, will hasten the day of Jesus' return."

Endnotes

[1] The World Book Encyclopedia – Volume 4 p. 45 2m

[2] Apostle Elizabeth Hairston – Cities have personalities; therefore, it is good to define the meaning of cities to comprehend the purposes and history, which a city possesses. This helps one to see how Apostles' presence in cities can cause conflict, yet change. Note the meanings and character of the cities, which Abram's travel impacted as he searched for the city with godly principles and precepts.

[3] Apostle Elizabeth A. Hairston, PhD. – terminology used by author to be consistent with terms used in cities.

[4] Ibid.

[5] Ibid.

[6] New Illustrated Webster's Dictionary

[7] Flavius Josephus, Complete Works of Flavius Josephus, p. 29

[8] Ibid., p. 32

[9] Bob Beckett with Rebecca Wagner-Sytsema, Commitment to Conquer, p. 84.

[10] Apostle Elizabeth A. Hairston, PhD – Note: The meanings and character of the cities that Abram's travel impact as he searched for the city with godly principles and precepts.

[11] Merrill Unger, Unger's Bible Handbook, p. 63

[12] Lawrence O. Richards, Richards' Complete Bible Handbook, p. 72

[13] Flavius Josephus, Complete Works of Flavius Josephus, p. 56

[14] Merrill Unger, Unger's Bible Handbook, p. 89

[15] Flavius Josephus, Complete Works of Flavius Josephus, p. 620

[16] Apostle Elizabeth Hairston – Legion = 6,000, literally an army

[17] Ronald F. Youngblood, Nelson New Illustrated Bible Dictionary, p. 235.

[18] Ibid, p. 984

[19] The Quest Study Bible, p. 1530

[20] Charles Trombley, Who Said Women Can't Preach?, p. 190

[21] Ibid., p. 191

[22] Frieda C. White, A Woman Called To Preach?, p. 49

[23] John MacArthur, The MacArthur Study Bible NKJV, p. 1724

[24] Trent C. Butler, PhD, Holman Bible Dictionary, p. 454

[25] Jane C. McFann, Reading Today, p. 1 of 4

[26] Ibid, p. 2 of 4

[27] Nell Irvin Painter, <u>Sojourner Truth</u>, p. 12

[28] Ibid, p. 34

[29] Ibid, p. 75

[30] Ibid, p. 126

[31] Richard L. Green, <u>A Salute to Historic Black Women</u> Empak Enterprises, Inc. p. 24

[32] Marcy Heidish, <u>A Woman Called Moses</u>, p. 305 (Under Author's Note)

[33] Negro Spiritual – Public Domain

[34] <u>Notable American Women…A Biographical Dictionary</u>, p. 482

[35] Richard Green, <u>A Salute To Historic Women</u>, p. 24

[36] A'Lelia Bundles, <u>On Her Own Ground – The Life and Times of Madam C. J. Walker</u>, p. 15

[37] Ibid, p. 45

[38] Ibid, p. 59

[39] Ibid, p. 20

[40] Richard Green, <u>A Salute To Historic Women</u>, p. 6

[41] Christine Lunardini, PhD, <u>What Every American Should Know About Women's History</u>, p. 236

Bibliography

1. Beckett, Bob and Sytsema, Rebecca Wagner. <u>Commitment To Conquer: Redeeming Your City By Strategic Intercession.</u> Grand Rapids, Michigan: Chosen Books, A Division of Baker House Company, 1997.

2. Bundles, A'Lelia. <u>On Her Own Ground: The Life and Times of Madam C. J. Walker.</u> New York, New York: A Lisa Drew Book, 2001.

3. Butler, Trent C., PhD, General Editor. <u>Holman Bible Dictionary</u>. Nashville, Tennessee: Holman Bible Publishers, 1991.

4. Edward T. James and Janet Wilson-James, Editors. <u>Notable American Women 1607–1950 A Biographical Dictionary.</u> Cambridge, Massachusetts: Harvard University Press, 1974.

5. Green, Richard L. and Dorothy M. Love-Carroll, Editors. <u>A Salute to Historic Black Women.</u> Chicago, Illinois: Empak Enterprises, Inc., 1966

6. Hairston, PhD. Elizabeth A. Apostle. City Language – Terminology used by the author to be consistent with terms used in cities.

7. Heidish, Marcy. <u>Woman Called Moses: A Novel Based On The Life Of Harriet Tubman.</u> Boston, Massachusetts: Houghton Mifflin Company, 1976.

8. <u>The Holy Bible: New International Version.</u> Grand Rapids, Michigan: Zondervan Publishing House, 1984.

9. Josephus, Flavius. <u>Complete Works of Flavius Josephus.</u> Grand Rapids, Michigan: Kregel Publications, 1981.

10. Lunardini, Christine, PhD <u>What Every American Should Know About Women's History: 200 Events That Shaped Our Destiny.</u> Holbrook, Massachusetts: Adams Media Corporation, 1994.

11. MacArthur, Jr. John F. The MacArthur Study Bible: New King James Version. Nashville, Tennessee: Word Publishing, 1977.

12. McFann, Jane. "When I Can Read My Title Clear: Literarcy, Slavery, And Religion In The Antebellum South." (Periodical) Reading Today. South Carolina: University of South Carolina Press, 1991.

13. Negro Spiritual "Steal Away" – Public Domain.

14. New Illustrated Webster's Dictionary of the English Language. New York, New York: Pamco Publishings Company, Inc. 1992.

15. Painter, Nell Irvin. Sojourner Truth: A Life, A Symbol. New York, New York: W. W. Norton and Company, Inc., 1997.

16. The Quest Study Bible: New International Version. Grand Rapids, Michigan: Zondervan Publishing House, 1994.

17. Richardson, Lawrence O. and Richards, Larry. Richard's Complete Bible Handbook. New York, New York: W. Publishing Group, 1987.

18. Trombley, Charles, Who Said Women Can't Teach? South Plainfield, New Jersey: Bridge-Logos Publishers, Inc., 1985.

19. Unger, Merrill F., Th.D., PhD Unger's Bible Handbook: An Essential Guide To Understanding The Bible. Chicago, Illinois: Moody Press, 1967.

20. White, Freida Carter, A Woman Called to Preach? Cleveland, Ohio: House of Manna Publications, 1978.

21. The World Book Encyclopedia. Danbury, Connecticut: World Book, Inc., 1985.

22. Youngblood, Ronald T. and Bruce, F. F., Editors. Nelson New Illustrated Bible Dictionary. Nashville, Tennessee: Thomas Nelson Publishers, 1996.

Additional Books
By The Author

Apostle Elizabeth A. Hairston, PhD.

P. O. Box 541564
Opa-Locka, Florida 33054

Telephone: (305) 654-9059
E-mail: Aposprop@bellsouth.net

House Cleaning In Bethel

The Strategies and Dynamics of Praise and Worship

Gates of Freedom

A Dove Upon My Shoulder

Go Forth In Dance

Printed in the United States
32057LVS00003B/13-22

9 781594 674044